This book is dedicated to
those who have suffered
and continue to suffer
because of bullying.

No learning can take place
when our children are not safe.

Table of Contents

Perfect Targets: Asperger Syndrome and Bullying

Practical Solutions for Surviving the Social World

Rebekah Heinrichs

With Foreword by Brenda Smith Myles

Autism Asperger Publishing Co.
P.O. Box 23173
Shawnee Mission, Kansas 66283-0173
www.asperger.net

2003 by Autism Asperger Publishing Co.
P.O. Box 23173
Shawnee Mission, Kansas 66283-0173
www.asperger.net

Publisher's Cataloging-in-Publication
(provided by Quality Books, Inc.)

Heinrichs, Rebekah.
　　Perfect targets : Asperger syndrome and bullying :
practical solutions for surviving the social world /
Rebekah Heinrichs ; with foreword by Brenda Smith Myles.
　　p. cm.
Includes bibliographical references and index.
LCCN 2003110483
ISBN 1-931282-18-8

　　1. Bullying in schools–Prevention. 2. Asperger's
syndrome. 3. Autistic children–Education.　I. Title.

LB3013.3.H45 2003　　　　371.7'82
　　　　　　　　　　QBI03-200618

Cover Design: Dianne Waldo
Cover Photo: Sherry L. Skinner
Cover Model: Kyle Skinner
Managing Editor: Kirsten McBride
Production Assistance: Ginny Biddulph
Interior Design/Production: Tappan Design

Foreword

Brenda Smith Myles

On a recent visit to a nearby elementary school, I had some time to spare while waiting for an appointment and elected to spend it on the school playground on a beautiful spring morning. My attention was soon caught by Sandy, a 9-year-old girl with Asperger Syndrome (AS). Sandy was surrounded by three girls – all busily talking. Although the three girls were smiling and laughing, it was difficult from my vantage point to tell what they were saying. As I moved closer, I heard the girls telling Sandy that it would be really funny if she snug into the classroom early and put a tack on their homeroom teacher's chair, Ms. Carlson. This was clearly no sudden impulse; the girls were ready – before Sandy even had time to respond, they gave her a tack and egged her on, saying that everyone in the class would laugh and think she was great if Ms. Carlson sat on the tack.

I normally don't intercede in schools I visit, but when no other adult moved to the group, I stepped forward. In a stern voice, I told the girls that what they were doing was inappropriate and that I was going to report them to the principal. I added that it is never okay to do something to a teacher or other person that can hurt them. While the three girls were very upset that they had been caught, Sandy appeared puzzled, almost disappointed at the turn of events. After escorting the group, including Sandy, to the office, I explained the situation to the principal, who promptly asked the three girls to come into his office.

As Sandy and I walked back to her classroom, she appeared very upset. When I asked what was wrong, she blamed me for having ruined her friendship with the girls. When I tried to explain that true friends do not set up their friends like this, Sandy responded, although somewhat subdued, that they were her friends because they usually talked to her during recess!

This type of heartbreaking and cruel scenario is a frequent occurrence in the lives of children and youth with Asperger Syndrome, making them feel less than adequate, confused, or upset, sometimes with lifelong consequences. Failing to understand that they are being bullied, some, like

Sandy, follow the group that hurts them or prompts them to do something inappropriate out of a desperate wish just to belong and have "friends."

Bullying has reached epidemic proportions nationwide among children and youth with AS. Tragically, it is so common that some children with AS, like Sandy, consider bullying a typical part of their day! It is a very sad reflection on our society that a book like this is necessary. However, given the realities of the daily lives of children and youth with AS in schools and in neighborhoods, it is probably one of the books most needed by these children, their parents, and teachers.

In this powerful book, Rebekah has addressed the silent epidemic of bullying in a manner that is both truthful and compassionate. With a large dose of objectivity, she identifies the various types of bullying, holding both adults and bullies accountable. Unlike some other bullying programs, she does not make the students with AS responsible for protecting themselves from bullying, recognizing that the persons being bullied have the least power and, therefore, few options with which to protect themselves, including friends who can stand up for them. Interspersing poignant stories of children and adults with AS who have been victimized, Rebekah offers practical solutions to the bullying at the schoolwide, classroom, and individual level. Throughout, special attention is paid to the unique characteristics of individuals with AS that make them more vulnerable than most to this cruel form of behavior.

Among the numerous books I have read, I believe this is the most socially valid and significant on this topic. In writing this much-needed resource, Rebekah has made a significant contribution to the lives of children and youth with AS and their parents, as well as added to the repertoire of strategies teachers and school leaders can use to stem the tide of bullying. *Perfect Targets* will positively impact individuals with AS and help them feel safe in their school and community – for some, perhaps for the first time!!

– Brenda Smith Myles, Ph.D., Associate Professor,
University of Kansas
Author (with colleagues), *Asperger Syndrome and Difficult Moments: Practical Solutions for Tantrums, Rage, and Meltdowns; Asperger Syndrome and Adolescence: Practical Solutions for School Success; Asperger Syndrome and Sensory Issues: Practical Solutions for Making Sense of the World;* and *Asperger Syndrome: A Guide for Educators and Parents*

Acknowledgments

This book became a reality because of the encouragement and support of my mentor and friend, Brenda Smith Myles. She made me believe I could write this book and convinced me that it would make a difference.

I also want to thank my mother, Sally Leffler, who did laundry, cleaned, cooked, and generally took good care of our family so I could spend time researching and writing. Thanks also go out to Harold, Sam, and Jillian for being the best cheering section anyone could ask for. Jillian was especially willing to share a "typical" teenager's point of view. The encouragement of friends, family, and many others kept me motivated.

Special thanks to Kirsten McBride, who is everything an editor should be and more. I consider myself fortunate to have benefited from her guidance and support.

Thanks to everyone who took the time to share their insights and experiences about bullying, especially Officer Randy Wiler with the Kansas Bullying Prevention Program; Dr. Richard Howlin of Chelsea, Michigan; Ruth Zweifler and the Student Advocacy Center of Michigan; Miranda and her mom; Benjamin and his mom; and Peter Myers.

Finally, I want to thank my own lifelong "best friends," who arrived at my side on cue when I really needed a friend and have remained true friends throughout the years. Kathy Dooley, who befriended me when I moved in the eighth grade and was by my side throughout high school; Vicki Spradlin, who met me on the first day of college orientation and helped me "decide which roads to take" and who remains one of my dearest friends; Karen Bickel, with whom I have shared pregnancies, balancing career and family, and personal passions (quilting); Dianne Waldo, who made me want to return to Kansas when I was "not in Kansas anymore;" Elisa Gagnon, who convinced me to return to school and encouraged me every step of the way; and Brenda Myles, first a role model, advisor, and mentor, and now first and foremost, my friend.

– Rebekah Heinrichs

PART ONE

Understanding Bullying

CHAPTER 1

Let's Put Bullying Into Perspective

Cameron's Story

Cameron in the following example is an 11-year-old boy with a diagnosis of Asperger Syndrome (AS). Because of his social naïvety, he is easily manipulated into a situation where he is hurt both physically and emotionally.

> Cameron is getting ready to begin the fifth grade and is at school to pick up his supplies and to look at the class and teacher assignments. A boy named Ryan approaches him and asks him if he wants to go outside and wrestle. Ryan is a student who bullied Cameron a lot in the fourth grade. Cameron thinks it is odd that Ryan is being friendly to him but wants to be his friend, so he agrees to wrestle.
>
> Ryan is with his cousin, and together they lead Cameron to a secluded spot outside the school building where they know they won't be seen by anybody. While Cameron is reciting wrestling

rules, both boys jump him, knock him down, and begin hitting and choking him. Finally, they call him names and laugh at him as they leave.

Cameron is surprised and upset because he did not anticipate that they were going to hurt him. He also feels humiliated because he realizes he has been tricked. Cameron goes back inside the school, and when he sees Ryan's mom he tells her that Ryan just beat him up. She grabs Ryan roughly by the arm and quickly leaves without speaking to Cameron. When Cameron tells his mother what happened, she is naturally upset and insists that they meet with the principal. Cameron has obvious scratches, bruises, and marks on his neck. He is able to tell the principal in detail what happened. Later when the principal calls Ryan's parents, they present a very different story. They report that they believe all three boys were "roughhousing" and should all be held accountable for using bad judgment and wrestling on school property. Because there are no witnesses, the principal asks the boys to write a letter of apology for wrestling on school grounds, including Cameron. Cameron tells his Mom that Ryan probably thinks he can do whatever he wants now without getting in trouble. Cameron and his mom are both very upset, and she refuses to allow Cameron to write the letter of apology.

This is an unfortunate example of how vulnerable children with AS can be when targeted for bullying and how savvy some students are when bullying others. In this case, the student who is targeted (Cameron) no longer feels safe at school, and the students who bullied continue their aggressive patterns with little concern for consequences. In fact, the very next year in middle school, Ryan brags about "beating up" Cameron (something he denied the year before to the principal and his parents) and pays another student to beat Cameron up while he watches. Because the incident occurred after school, the middle school principal feels he cannot "punish" Ryan, but he does bring Ryan and the other student into his office and speaks to their parents. Even after the principal "puts Ryan and the other student on notice," they continue to verbally taunt and tease Cameron during school. Cameron no longer reports the bullying because he doesn't believe it will do any good.

This book will examine the phenomenon of bullying and recommend steps to be taken that will make a positive difference in the lives of our children. Throughout, I will consider the unique social challenges and needs of children with AS and offer insights and strategies that will empower adults to effectively provide for their safety. When appropriate, I will also include strategies that children can use to help prevent or counter bullying. All proposed strategies should be individualized based on the strengths and challenges of individual students, keeping in mind that *adults* are ultimately the changing force behind any effective bullying prevention program.

In this chapter I discuss the pervasiveness of bullying in schools today and how developmental and environmental factors impact these experiences. Also covered in this chapter is how children cope with bullying and the implications for children with AS. An overview of key components of successful bullying prevention programs is presented as well.

Bullying in Schools

What have we learned from the general research on bullying? There is relatively little research in the United States on bullying, but a surge of interest and awareness has emerged in recent years due, in part, to acts of violence in our schools and school shootings. Many government leaders, school administrators, and educators are now scrambling to develop bullying prevention policies and programs.

Bullying Research

Studies conducted in the United States confirm that bullying is a pervasive problem in our schools. Specifically, studies show bullying rates from 17% for middle school and high school students who are targets of moderate or frequent bullying (Nansel, Overpeck, Pilla, Ruan, Simon-Mortons, & Scheidt, 2001) to 75% for school-aged students who report being bullied at least once during the school year (Hoover, Oliver, & Hazler, 1992). Every school day, 160,000 (!) students miss school because they are afraid of being bullied (Fried & Fried, 1996). A recent large research study reported that 29.9% of children in grades 6 through 10 in public and private schools reported moderate or frequent involvement in bullying – 13% as a bully, 10.6 targeted by bullies, and 6.3% as both (Nansel et al., 2001). According to anecdotal reports, nearly all students say they have been teased and harassed at school (National Association of Attorneys General, 2000). This means that most children attending school in the United States experience bullying to some degree, and at least a third directly experience moderate to frequent involvement in bullying incidents.

For some students, bullying experiences are severe, chronic, and frequent. Approximately 10-15% of children who are targeted for bullying fall into this high-risk group. A smaller proportion (5-10%) are so seriously targeted that they require significant support from adults and peers to overcome their experiences and progress positively (Pepler & Craig, 2000).

Research also suggests that peers are almost always present when bullying occurs. This includes students who witness bullying and others who are more directly involved. Based on this research, 90% of children who witness bullying find it unpleasant and disturbing to watch (O'Connel, Pepler, & Craig, 1999). Therefore, in essence, all children are affected by bullying in their schools, making it even more important to come up with effective preventive and intervention approaches.

Bullying and Children with Special Needs

As a group, children with special needs are frequent targets of bullying. Kids who talk, act, or think differently tend to suffer more bullying and exclusion than someone with a physical challenge. There seems to be less tolerance and understanding of disabilities that are more hidden. Children, and sometimes adults, have a more difficult time understanding differences that they cannot see and, therefore, tend to misinterpret behaviors and have less empathy for children with other than physical challenges (Kavale & Forness, 1996; Little, 2002; Salmon, James, & Smith, 1998). For example, children with AS often make statements that are interpreted as rude because of their social deficits and literal interpretations. Because most children with AS are average to gifted in intelligence and look "normal," peers and even adults often have little tolerance for this characteristic manifestation of their disorder.

Bullying and Children with Asperger Syndrome

There is astonishingly little research on bullying and children with AS. In one of the existing studies, Little (2002) surveyed over 400 parents of children diagnosed with AS and nonverbal learning disability

(NLD), ranging in age from 4-17 years old, about bullying. Ninety-four percent of the parents responded that a peer had bullied their child at least once in the previous year. Compared to studies of the general population, kids with AS were four times more likely to be bullied, twice as likely to be hit or kicked in their privates, and twice as likely to be hit by their peers and siblings. These are truly astonishing statistics.

The results of the survey also indicated that children with AS and NLD experience high levels of peer shunning that seem to increase with age and peak in high school. Middle school is a time when most children are trying to fit in and not be noticed as being "different." Also, middle and high school are times when peers are more important and peer pressure influences much of what is considered "socially appropriate behavior." Because children with AS stand out and are alone more often than their typical peers, they are at greater risk for bullying and shunning at a time when peer acceptance is most critical.

Because children with AS stand out and are alone more often than their typical peers, they are at greater risk for bullying and shunning at a time when peer acceptance is most critical.

Peer shunning is the act of ignoring or excluding children. Examples include children who sit alone at lunch, who are picked last for activities or games, and who are not invited to birthday parties or other common social events. Little (2002) noted that 11% of the children in the study often ate lunch alone at school, 35% had not been invited to a birthday party in the last year, and 31% were habitually picked last for team activities. The study results clearly revealed that peer victimizations and bullying of all kinds are pervasive among children diagnosed with AS.

Ask most parents of children with AS, and they will tell you that these statistics do not surprise them at all. They may even wonder whether they underestimate the problem of bullying among children with AS. When I recently presented these findings to a group of parents at a support group meeting in Ann Arbor, Michigan, a mother immediately expressed surprise that 100% of the children in the study were not bullied. The rest of the group nodded their approval. No wonder, then, that for parents of a child diagnosed with AS one of the major worries is bullying and teasing of their child. It seems to be a universal experience for children with AS. The stories and experiences of bullying shared by parents and their children are typically chronic, frequent in occurrence and, too often, severe in nature.

Maria in the following example has a diagnosis of AS. Because she is socially naïve and has social-communication deficits, she is tricked into fulfilling a ridiculous request and, as a result, is mistakenly disciplined by the supervising teacher and school counselor. This situation is characteristic of the peer shunning she routinely experiences.

> *Maria is anxious to make friends with some of the popular girls in her fifth-grade class. At lunchtime, Nani, a very popular girl, invites Maria to sit with her and some of the other popular girls. This has never happened before, so Maria is extremely excited and jumps at the chance to be included. Unknown to Maria, Nani is upset with her friend Hannah, who usually sits at the table. When Hannah arrives with her lunch tray, Nani calmly and quietly instructs Maria to tell Hannah that she cannot sit at their table because she has been replaced for the day. Maria complies, and Hannah begins to cry. This draws the attention of the supervising teacher, who quickly learns from Hannah what Maria said to her. Maria is sent to the office where the counselor asks her to write down what she did on a Bullying Incident Form. In addition, the counselor talks to Maria about how important it is to remember the class rule about including others.*

> *The next day Nani and Hannah have made up with each other, and things are back to normal: The popular girls sit together and Maria sits alone at the table unofficially reserved for kids who are never asked to join a group and who find "saved seats" whenever they attempt to join in with others.*

Maria had difficulty interpreting this social experience and was not able to identify that she was being targeted. When she met with the counselor, she could not adequately verbalize her feelings and thoughts because of her confusion about what had happened. Many children with AS face similar challenges related to social interactions. Children who bully, however, are often very adept at discerning the vulnerabilities of their targets. Whenever a child with AS is involved in social incidents, it is difficult to sort out what has actually occurred.

Children with AS are at considerable risk for serious, long-lasting consequences due to the intensity and frequency of their bullying experiences. School is a major social arena for all children, but particularly so for children with AS, since school is where most of their social experiences take place. Yet sadly, because of bullying and peer shunning, children with AS may be excluded from many of the activities that commonly make up the social lives of our children. Without an enormous amount of support and intervention coordinated by adults, these children will continue to be harassed by their peers.

Now let us explore what bullying looks like at different developmental stages. Bullying is not just a "kid" issue but a problem throughout the lifespan.

Looking at Bullying From a Developmental Perspective

We need to take bullying seriously and dispel myths such as "kids will just grow out of it" or "it is just a stage," along with other false beliefs. Based on their extensive research on bullying, Pepler and Craig (2000) take a developmental perspective, viewing bullying as a serious problem throughout the lifespan.

Different types of aggression and bullying are found according to developmental stage, including childhood, adolescence, and late adolescence. During childhood (ages 4-9 years), children typically exhibit verbal and/or physical aggression toward same-sex peers. During adolescence (ages 10-13 years), aggression is extended to opposite-sex peers, and more social and other types of bullying are seen. Further, sexual harassment may occur between same-sex *and* opposite-sex peers. In late adolescence (ages 14-18 years), romantic relationships factor in and date violence becomes a concern. In addition, gang behavior and delinquency in school and in the larger community become significant concerns as well (Pepler & Craig, 2000).

In taking a developmental view of bullying, it is important to consider how power and aggression are viewed throughout the lifespan. Bullying behaviors that occur during childhood can progress to other types of abuse later in life, such as child abuse, domestic violence, and bullying in the workplace, if new behaviors and patterns are not developed. Children who bully learn that power and aggression lead to attention, dominance, and increased status with some of their peers. The lesson learned is that those with power can be aggressive and being aggressive can be used to obtain what you want. We have reason to be concerned that these patterns of behavior may contribute to more serious types of bullying or violence using power and aggression in adulthood (Pepler & Craig, 2000).

Looking at bullying from an environmental perspective is also important. Next I will discuss the different factors in our environment that impact bullying.

Looking at Bullying From an Environmental Perspective

Thinking about bullying from an environmental perspective helps promote understanding of all the complex factors that play a role in bullying. I find a visual support helpful in understanding this point of view (see Figure 1.1). Although the characteristics of children relative to their language, cognition, social competence, and physical health are important, the social and physical environment they live in also impacts their behaviors and attitudes. Thus, family, school, peers, community, and cultural environments all play a role in determining whether children learn and whether they inhibit antisocial behaviors and develop prosocial behaviors.

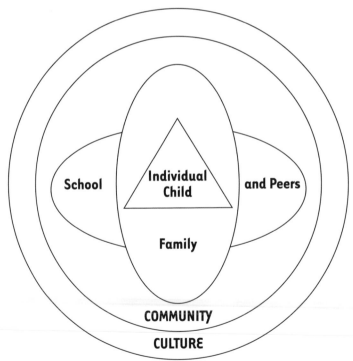

Figure 1.1. Conceptualization of bullying from an environmental perspective.

Central to bullying is the individual child. The triangle in the middle of Figure 1.1 represents the individual characteristics of the child and is a visual reminder of Maslow's hierarchy of needs (Maslow, 1987). Briefly, according to Maslow, every human has a hierarchy of needs and in order to move up to the next level, most of the needs in the lower level must be adequately met. Maslow (1987) uses a triangle to represent the different levels of needs. From bottom to top, they are physiological needs, safety and security, love and belonging, self-esteem, and lastly self-actualization.

As a result of Maslow's conceptualization, we now understand that children cannot learn if they are sick or hungry, do not get enough sleep, or are too cold. By the same token, we also need to understand that children cannot concentrate on learning if they do not feel safe or, in fact, are not safe at school! Children with AS are typically more anxious in general, and specifically more anxious in social situations. Their social-communication disability puts them at considerable risk for negative social interactions. Because of their increased anxiety, negative experiences, and inability to predict what will happen in social situations, children with AS hover closer to the edge of the "safety line" and, therefore, feel unsafe at school a significant portion of the time. Knowing this, we need to provide additional supports for children with AS so they do not have to expend so much energy trying to feel safe – energy that is not available to them for learning.

How Children Cope with Bullying in Schools

Recent research on bullying experiences in school has explored the social world of students and discovered that our children do not feel safe (Garbarino & deLara, 2002; National Association of Attorneys General, 2000; Rigby, 1996). Through their work with teenagers, Garbarino and deLara (2002) discovered that typical teenagers do not feel safe in school and that the main coping mechanism used by these students to feel safe is trying to predict the behavior of their peers and teachers. That is, when students can predict someone's behavior, they feel they will be safer by knowing how to stay out of harm's way. This includes predicting which areas in school are "unowned spaces" that should be avoided – places that are typically less supervised and are identified by students as being more dangerous and potentially unsafe. Examples of "unowned spaces" include bathrooms, certain out-of the-way hallways, locker rooms, and other areas, depending on the physical layout of the school building (Garbarino & deLara, 2002).

Garbarino and deLara (2002) concluded that students are "over-functioning" trying to stay safe in school while the adults are "under-functioning." So much energy is being expended on trying to predict behaviors in order to feel safe that it is detracting from students' ability to learn. This is intolerable. Adults need to take more responsibility for providing a safe learning environment so children can attend to the task of learning.

Implications for Children with Asperger Syndrome

If typical students are spending an inordinate amount of time and energy trying to predict behaviors so that they can be safe, we can safely assume that children with AS expend even more energy predicting behavior. More important, because of their difficulty taking the perspective of others or predicting what they may be thinking or feeling in social situations (theory of mind), children with AS are greatly disadvantaged in this respect. As a result, they spend a tremendous amount of time and energy trying to predict behaviors with very little success.

Typical students learn who not to talk back to (teachers and students), who not to playfully tease or joke with, what times to avoid the hall by the library, and which kids are less predictable and/or aggressive and therefore need to be avoided. Accumulating a variety of information from different sources and generalizing to future situations is how students make these types of predictions.

But students with AS are characteristically poor at picking up on social cues and reading into social situations. They also have difficulty taking social information from one situation and generalizing it to other situations. This puts them at a distinct disadvantage when trying to predict the behavior of others and makes it more difficult for them to feel safe at school and at a higher risk for negative social interactions.

Students with AS are characteristically poor at picking up on social cues and reading into social situations.

No wonder children with AS often have such high levels of anxiety and still end up experiencing pervasive bullying. And no wonder that many children with AS express negative feelings about school.

Dr. Richard Howlin, a private therapist in Chelsea, Michigan, specializes in working with individuals diagnosed with AS and related disabilities. He states, "The common thread in every child, adolescent, or adult I have worked with diagnosed with AS is that they all express that they hate or hated school." As we work to identify the dynamics behind the negative school experiences of many children with AS, bullying prevention and intervention must be an important part of this process.

Bullying Prevention

How do we address the issue of bullying in our schools? One approach, zero tolerance, is becoming a standard in most schools.

Zero Tolerance

All over the United States, zero tolerance policies are becoming the norm. Zero tolerance policies were embraced as a result of the federal Gun-Free Schools Act of 1994 in an effort to comply with the mandate that all states require at least a one-year expulsion for carrying firearms on school property or risk losing federal funding. The local educational agency is required to provide a description of the circumstances of the expulsion (name of school, students expelled, and type of weapons involved) to their state to be compiled in a report and sent to the United States Department of Education. However, many states have not complied with the reporting provision. This is a dangerous practice, with schools expelling students without adequate monitoring. Such lack of monitoring decreases accountability and limits our ability to adequately evaluate a policy that seriously impacts the lives of many students (Polakow-Suransky, 1999; U.S. Code, 1994).

Zero tolerance was started in 1994 as a way of getting guns out of school. One year later the act was revised to expand the prohibition to weapons rather than just firearms. This opened the door for more discretion in terms of what could be construed as a dangerous weapon, and with that an increased possibility of discriminatory practices. In fact, there have been many highly publicized cases in which students have been expelled for bringing something as innocuous as a fingernail clipper to school, including extremely young students who bring items to school that bear little resemblance to real weapons with no intent to do harm. Even though the federal law leaves room for extenuating circumstances and provides for schools to determine that an expulsion is not warranted, many schools choose not to venture into this area for fear of legal repercussions from the families involved. Instead, the tendency has been for schools to go beyond the provisions of federal law by enacting policies that mandate suspensions or expulsions for a variety of student behaviors (Ayers, Dohrn, & Ayers, 2001; Polakow-Suransky, 1999).

Our schools are becoming more like prisons, placing our children into the juvenile and adult criminal courts as we criminalize more and more behaviors out of fear, instead of working on the underlying issues and increasing adult accountability. Few will argue about the importance of zero tolerance for guns in school, but the way zero tolerance policies are being implemented has often led to a "one-size-fits-all" mandatory punishment that we can no longer afford to embrace (Ayers et al., 2001).

As a result of zero tolerance policies, more and more children all over the United States are becoming victims of arbitrary suspensions and expulsions with their educational futures left hanging in the balance. Even for students who clearly need some kind of intervention, often there are no options but to remain out of school due to a lack of alternative educational opportunities. Some of the reasons for suspension or expulsion include behaviors related to bullying such as physical violence, fighting, carrying a weapon with intent to harm or as protection from bullies, verbal threats of violence, and even violent drawings or written expressions with violent content.

What about the child who is being bullied and finally reacts in response to his treatment? Surely, the answer is not to "wash our hands" and send everyone home. Bullying is a serious issue in our schools that needs to be addressed by thinking adults willing to invest the time and energy necessary to change attitudes and behaviors. We must not allow zero tolerance to evolve into "zero thinking" out of fear – fear of lawsuits, school shootings, and unfortunately, fear of our very own children.

We must be diligent in how we define and address bullying in our schools. Although bullying is not against the law in the United States, we do have laws against hate crimes and sexual harassment. As a result, schools are given the task of discriminating the boundaries between these various types of behaviors. In the current, sometimes alarmist, discussions of bullying, there is a tendency to define as bullying everything from rolling your eyes once at someone to blatant sexual abuse.

We need to make sure that we do not err too far in either direction. Common sense must be part of the process, while ensuring that we do not let old beliefs and attitudes allow bullying behaviors to go unchecked. For example, we can no longer afford to excuse name-calling as "kids will be kids" when the consequences of such behaviors are harmful and sometimes result in serious outcomes such as depression and children who refuse to go to school.

A Better Approach to Bullying Prevention

Our children have a right to a safe learning environment free from violence, and schools are required to do their best to provide such an environment. We cannot expect the least empowered person, the targeted child, to bear the burden of "beating the bullies" or to somehow figure out how to change his or her behavior in order to create a safer school environment. This is particularly true when children with AS are involved, because compared to their neurotypical peers, their social-communication disability renders them more at risk for bullying and at the same time makes them less skilled at effectively protecting themselves when bullying occurs. Bullying is a serious issue with serious consequences and adults must take the lead in creating a school environment where bullying is neither valued nor accepted. Effective bullying prevention programs need to involve the entire community and include steps at the school, class, and individual level. There is no easy answer or "quick fix."

When looking at bullying prevention, we must use the best proven strategies that research has to offer instead of trying to predict what might work or creating harsh policies in an effort to remove the "bad apples."

Relatively little research on bullying prevention has been conducted in the United States, but a larger body of research is available in other countries. For example, Olweus (1993) of Norway is a pioneer in bullying research and intervention. He has developed a thoroughly tested and researched whole-school bullying prevention program that most other bullying programs emulate, at least in part. Time, staff, funding, and other resources are typically stretched to the limits in most schools. Recognizing this, Olweus has identified vital "core components" for bullying prevention programs (p. 121):

1. Adult awareness and involvement
2. A questionnaire survey
3. Effective supervision during breaks
4. Educational teacher discussion groups
5. The formation of a coordinating group
6. Class rules against bullying
7. Class meetings with students
8. Serious talks with bullies and targets
9. Serious talks with parents of involved students

Olweus' environmental approach to bullying has been empirically validated. For example, he noted marked reductions of 50% or more in bullying problems during the two years following the introduction of the programs with over 2,500 students (Olweus, 1993).

We must be careful when transferring research conducted in other countries and cultures to the diverse population in the United States. However, experts in the United States and elsewhere have embraced Olweus' program as a model program. Olweus encourages schools to include as many key components as possible while individualizing strategies according to the unique needs and resources of the school population. For instance, if a school is unable to incorporate weekly class meetings to discuss bullying issues, a different meeting frequency can be chosen based on available school resources and time restrictions. The most important requirement is that there be an ongoing scheduled commitment to providing a forum for students and adults to dialogue about bullying.

Zero tolerance policies and punitive measures alone do not adequately address bullying in our schools. In fact, they exacerbate the problem by failing to address the complex factors that make up the often subtle dynamics of bully-target interactions. Besides, research has shown that bullying touches the lives of almost all children in our schools. Zero tolerance and an emphasis on punitive measures serve to create a culture of silence and fear where children are too frightened and anxious to talk about their experiences or, worse yet, make children feel they are expected to behave perfectly and are denied their educational experience when they are unable to comply. Are we to hold our children to a higher level of accountability than we experience as adults? If an adult were to verbally threaten another adult, he or she would have considerable protection under the law before being held accountable for his or her actions. However, if a student verbally threatens a teacher or student, many school policies provide that they can be suspended or even expelled at the discretion of the school administration.

What lesson do we teach our children when we deny them even the most basic of civil rights – rights that are denied under the application of zero tolerance policies and punitive measures that are sometimes arbitrary and too often discriminatory?

Key Components of Successful Bullying Prevention Programs

Successful bullying prevention programs must include a strong emphasis on awareness and understanding as well as formative and/or prosocial consequences. Formative discipline includes consequences that teach or help a child think in a different way, and those that challenge and change behavior as opposed to being mere punitive measures. Prosocial discipline provides consequences where a child is required to do something positive and then receives positive feedback in response (Garrity et al., 2000). In all these efforts, it is imperative that adults take more responsibility.

All or most of the key components listed in Table 1.1 must be included in a successful bullying prevention program.

TABLE 1.1

Key Components of a Successful Bullying Prevention Program

- Increase awareness and understanding
- Gather information from teachers, students, and parents (surveys)
- Create a coordinating group (include school staff, students, and parents)
- Develop a school and class code
- Provide staff training
- Conduct class meetings with students
- Increase supervision in high-risk areas with proactive, trained adults
- Have adults model appropriate behaviors
- Apply formative and/or prosocial consequences
- Promote social competence skills for targets, bullies, and bystanders
- Involve the parents of students in bully-target incidents, including bystanders
- Modify bullying prevention interventions as needed for students with exceptionalities

---

Adapted from Olweus, D. (1993). *Bullying at school: What we know and what we can do.* Oxford: Blackwell Publishers, p. 127.

It is essential that modifications be integrated into prevention programs as necessary to successfully meet the requirements of children with special needs; especially children diagnosed with AS or other pervasive developmental disorders. These children are the most vulnerable to bullying and require significant support from adults. We are required by law to provide a safe environment for every child in the school community.

In the next chapter I will define bullying, explore the different types of bullying, discuss implications for children with AS related to bullying, and finally, highlight the importance of a team approach to bullying prevention.

CHAPTER 2

What Is Bullying?

Juan's Story

The following scenario reflects a situation that a seventh-grade boy diagnosed with Asperger Syndrome (AS) experienced in art class at a public middle school in a Midwest suburban community.

> *Juan has been teased a lot this year. The school administrators have identified a group of kids who are not to be seated near Juan in classes because of teasing and bullying issues. One of the boys even met Juan for a fight after school a few weeks ago and ended up hitting Juan several times, bruising his arms badly. Unfortunately, when the nine-week term ended and specials classes changed, the staff forgot to check who was in Juan's new specials class. As luck would have it, he was seated at a small table with some of these students, including the student who had physically assaulted him. This class was very hands-on and*

loosely structured, allowing for a lot of verbal interaction between students with little teacher supervision.

The first week Juan started to feel uncomfortable with some of the things students said to him but did not go to anyone for help. One day during the second week, he teased a boy in the group whom he did not know very well. Juan stated later that he just wanted to get some of the attention off of himself, and when the other students laughed and encouraged him, he kept talking. Juan found himself saying lots of things to the boy, encouraged by the other students at the table who kept telling him to "say something else." Suddenly the other students began to say things to the targeted boy like "I wouldn't take that off of him," and "Are you going to let him get away with that?" and finally, "If someone said that to me, I would hit him."

At no time did the teacher intervene even though the room was fairly small and she was sitting at a table directly behind the students with her back to the group of boys involved. Later the teacher stated that she heard them talking but was busy helping other students and, therefore, did not realize that the conversations were inappropriate. Also, she was not aware that there had been prior conflicts between the students.

In the hall immediately after class, Juan walked up to the boy he had targeted to apologize because he felt bad about some of the things he had said. But before Juan could say a word, the boy punched him in the face, knocking his glasses off. Juan did not go to his next class. Instead, he went to the room of his favorite teacher, his English teacher, who escorted him to the office so he could report what had happened. Almost the entire left side of Juan's face became bruised, with a considerable amount of swelling around his left eye. The bruising did not completely disappear for two weeks and Juan missed a week of school. At first he missed because of the pain and swelling, and then he was too humiliated to return until the swelling and bruising lessened. When Juan's parents went to speak to the resource police officer at the school, he told them that he had reason to believe that "some of the teachers felt Juan got what he deserved," adding, "maybe this isn't the right school for Juan."

What Went Wrong?

Looking at this unfortunate situation, we notice several factors that contributed to Juan's experiences. Obviously, there needs to be more teacher supervision during class and in the hallways. However, the underlying problem seems to be a lack of understanding of Juan's unique challenges and a general lack of awareness on the part of the teachers of the types of bullying and teasing that are going on right in their classrooms and hallways.

The administration failed to follow through and advocate for Juan despite his significant history of being targeted with verbal, social, and severe physical bullying. In other words, they dropped the ball in providing protection, so Juan was left to his own devices in a culture of "don't tell on anyone" to try to avoid being bullied. Juan thought he had found a good strategy because of the feedback he received from the other kids, but he did not recognize when he was being manipulated along with the student he targeted. The end result was harsh and dramatically impacted the rest of his year. Juan felt let down by the adults at his school and concluded they were not going to help him. He continued to experience frequent bullying for the rest of the year.

If this school had a bullying prevention plan in place with proactive, informed, and willing adults taking the lead, things might have gone much differently. In Juan's case, the teachers were not told about many of the incidents where Juan had been targeted for bullying. However, the teachers could not help but notice Juan's behaviors or reactions when he interacted with his peers, which led them to believe that he often intentionally provoked others. Many teachers were also frustrated with Juan's behavior in class as he often got in trouble for talking too much, getting off task, and being argumentative. All of these factors played a critical role in the outcome of Juan's situation even though his behaviors were a manifestation of his disability. A proactive plan for addressing bullying, effective communication, and better understanding of the challenges faced by Juan related to his social-communication disorder would have made all the difference in Juan's school experiences, and perhaps even have prevented this event altogether.

Establishing a foundation of understanding and awareness about bullying is critical. Also, unless teachers and other school staff are educated concerning the special challenges of children with AS related to peer interactions, and bullying specifically, they are unlikely to understand how high risk these children are for serious consequences as a result of chronic, frequent, and severe bullying. Children with AS need a lot of adult support and intervention if they are to be able to receive a free and appropriate public education because children who are frequently victimized do not feel safe and their ability to learn is impaired.

Defining Bullying

An integral part of developing a successful bullying prevention program involves reaching a consensus on how to define bullying and frank discussions about the types of bullying that occur in schools.

The definition of bullying includes some type of *power imbalance, intent to harm, a distressed target, and repeated negative actions.* Some type of power imbalance is typically present in bully-target incidents, and targets for bullying usually feel unable to respond effectively against the person or persons harassing them. We tend to think of the physically larger, older bully looming over a smaller, younger child. However, the power imbalance can be related to other factors, such as the physical presence of friends with the bully and the target being alone. It can also be a matter of social status, where the bully wields power and status in the school community (such as a school athlete) compared to the target, who may have relatively low social status.

The target may lack the social awareness and skills to effectively deal with negative peer interactions, whereas the bully may be quite capable in this area.

Social skills also play an important role in bullying. The target may lack the social awareness and skills to effectively deal with negative peer interactions, whereas the bully may be quite capable in this area. Bullies may also be skilled at talking their way out of difficult situations, which may help avoid consequences. In brief, *the power imbalance may be physical and/or psychological in nature.*

In situations where children with exceptionalities are targets, the power imbalance can be extremely exaggerated. This is particularly true for children diagnosed with AS because many of their deficits relate to the social arena. Although bullying typically involves repeated, negative actions, school staff and parents must remember always to consider the significant power imbalance that exists when children with AS are targets of bullying. It is also critical that adults understand how the individual challenges of children with AS can provide unique opportunities for bullying to occur and how bullying sometimes looks different when children with AS are involved. Because of their social naïvety and social-communication deficits, such as misinterpreting social and/or nonverbal communication, children with AS are easily manipulated and harmed. Adults may even misinterpret some bullying situations and end up punishing the child with AS because he or she has been so successfully set up. The following is an example of such an incident.

> *Michael is a 12-year-old with AS. He is often encouraged by a group of boys in his class to blurt out during class. For instance, the boys tell him to say something funny about the substitute teacher's baldness or to make fun of another kid in the class who is overweight. They encourage him by laughing, but they also tell on him and laugh when he gets in trouble. Michael thinks these boys are his friends, but they are just manipulating him for their own amusement.*

Also, some children with AS can become scapegoats for entire classes and therefore are targeted for bullying by children who otherwise do not exhibit bullying behaviors. The following relates the experiences of Paul. Paul is 15 years old and diagnosed with AS. He is in general education classes for most of the school day.

> *Paul is easily upset by changes in his schedule. At least twice a week, one of the other students in his class makes up a schedule change and, for example, tells him that they are going to have an unannounced test or that school will be dismissing early. Paul typically becomes upset and predictably goes from student to student in the class asking if what he has been told is true. He becomes more and more upset as every student confirms the "joke"; even students who would never dream of initiating bullying go along with the routine. Most students seem to be amused by Paul's predictable reactions and find it amazing that he falls for the same "joke" every time. They change the "joke" a little bit each time just to make sure they keep him guessing. Paul usually becomes so agitated that he ends up having to leave the room and go talk to his counselor for reassurance. Some of the students feel a little sorry for Paul but not enough to stand up for him. Still others find him annoying and are secretly relieved when he is out of the classroom.*

It is crucial that we recognize the many forms that bullying can take and the different roles that adults and students play in bully-target situations. While defining bullying is the first step in taking a proactive stance against bullying in our schools, it is even more important that we realize that the definition of bullying is ultimately describing a behavioral interaction, not just a person or a specific type of behavior.

Olweus (1993) describes bullying as a behavioral interaction. "A student is being bullied or victimized when he or she is exposed, repeatedly and over time, to negative actions on the part of one or more other students" (p. 9). This definition recognizes the infinite array of circumstances and influences that can contribute to bullying behaviors, such as previous experiences between participants in the interaction and the variety of methods or means by which these negative actions can be delivered.

Olweus does not include intention as a requirement in his definition. Although bullying incidents are typically intentional, there may be times when negative actions are repeated without specific intent to harm but are still considered bullying. An example is the use of sarcasm by a teacher to achieve a desired result in the classroom, such as controlling a student's behavior. As a result, the student experiences embarrassment and distress, and therefore harm is done whether intentional or not. This is sometimes characterized as "non-malign" bullying (Rigby, 1996, p. 17). I refer to this type of bullying as educational bullying and will examine it later in this chapter.

We need to use our definitions of bullying as a guideline, not a requirement, and look at the unique characteristics and circumstances of each situation. Bullying is a complex issue and must be dealt with in a comprehensive, thoughtful way.

Types of Bullying

Bullying is typically either physical, verbal, social, or educational. A variety of methods are used to bully. Basically, bullying is either delivered in a direct or indirect manner. *Direct bullying* occurs in an up-front, open way. This does not mean the student will bully in front of the teacher but refers to the method of injuring the target. Direct bullying may include the use of physical contact, words, gestures, or facial expressions delivered in an "in-your-face" way. *Indirect bullying* is when a student is excluded from the social group, resulting in intentional exclusion or isolation. This is often done in a more secretive or "back-stabbing" way and includes gossiping and intentionally trying to damage relationships. Peer shunning is a type of indirect bullying (Olweus, 1993; Pepler & Craig, 1999).

Physical Bullying

Many adults characterize most bullying as being physical, but this is a myth. In truth, physical bullying comprises the minority of bullying activity. Both boys and girls much more commonly experience verbal, social, and educational bullying. Nevertheless, physical bullying is a serious issue in our schools and one with potentially devastating, even fatal results.

Physical bullying includes hitting, pushing, tripping, kicking, spitting on someone, pulling hair, shouldering, grabbing clothes, belongings or parts of a person's body, and so forth. Because we are dealing with children, even when these direct, hands-on types of bullying occur, they are often ignored or written off as just "horsing around." Although girls can physically bully others, boys conduct the majority of physical bullying. Indeed, boys are more often both the targets and perpetrators of physical bullying (Olweus, 1993; Rigby, 1996).

Verbal Bullying

Verbal bullying includes teasing and making fun of someone, verbal threats, name-calling, and other types of incidents involving language. Obscene gestures, eye rolling, threatening stares, or other types of nonverbal communication are sometimes considered verbal bullying because they represent or replace words; others categorize these behaviors as physical because they involve the use of physical parts of the body. Still others refer to these types of nonverbal communications as social bullying because they are meant to intimidate or damage relationships. I believe that recognizing these bullying behaviors is more important than how we categorize them. Adults and students need to increase their level of awareness of verbal bullying and how hurtful and damaging it can be to those on the receiving end.

Even though girls are identified as using verbal bullying more often than boys, bullying by means of words, gestures, or other nonphysical means is also the most common form of bullying used by boys (Olweus, 1993; Rigby, 1996).

Verbal bullying and boys. Boys can be quite adept at verbal teasing, and many boys who exhibit verbal bullying behaviors excuse their teasing as something all kids should just be able to tolerate. Teasing among friends, especially boys, is common, but when asked, most children can explain the difference between playful teasing and teasing meant to hurt someone's feelings. When boys become uncomfortable with teasing, they generally give nonverbal cues such as lowering their eyebrows, lowering or raising the tone of their voice, and shifting their eyes to look at friends for backup. Sometimes their facial expression changes from fairly neutral to sad or angry, or they may begin laughing in an effort to counter the negative attention and hide their true feelings. Verbal teasing can escalate to physical violence, as the participants become more agitated by the content of the teasing language as in the scenario described earlier with Juan in art class.

Verbal bullying and girls. Several recent publications explore the nature and experience of girls related to verbal and social bullying. Most of the information is anecdotal due to the subject matter, but it is evident that verbal and social bullying is universal in our schools and that girls are major players in these types of relational behaviors. Girls are more likely to engage in group bullying involving peer shunning and manipulation of relationships (Simmons, 2002; White, 2002; Wiseman, 2002).

At a young age (up to age 4 years) girls show aggressive patterns similar to boys – they take toys away from their peers, they push and hit. Later, societal norms and expectations tend to cause girls' aggressions to become more cloaked, so they come out in less physical and visible ways. Girls often use information told in confidence to launch assaults and damage reputations. Because girls value intimacy and relationships and share so much personal information with each other, they possess the ability to be great friends and even worse enemies. Although some psychologists feel bonding is a motivation for some of these group bullying activities, others see it as a play for power within the social structure. The power theory would certainly relate to the definition of bullying where power and aggression are key factors (Talbot, 2002).

Verbal bullying and children with AS. Unfortunately, verbal bullying is an area where children with AS have difficulty identifying the social cues that could help them determine the intent behind these behaviors. Children with AS may have trouble evaluating whether someone is giving them social cues that they have crossed the line over to hurtful teasing and bullying when they try to model the teasing behavior of their peers. Children with AS are often caught up in unfortunate social situations where they are either frequently teased by others, or where they end up unintentionally hurting the feelings of others when trying out teasing behaviors they see other students successfully engage in.

Social Bullying

Social bullying occurs when the intent is to isolate or exclude someone from peers by spreading rumors, peer shunning, or other methods of damaging or manipulating relationships. This particularly damaging type of bullying can be quite devastating to both girls and boys, with girls being more likely to experience social bullying from groups (Olweus, 1993; Rigby, 1996).

The power imbalance present in social bullying is not necessarily physical, particularly with girls. Students who display bullying behaviors may be of a higher social standing, more assertive or verbally astute, have a powerful personality, and/or have a quick wit or tongue, helping them to easily ridicule or humiliate others. They may gain the help and support of others through persuasion or even persuasive threats. Girls who bully often threaten others with social exclusion if they do not support them in excluding or harassing their target. Acceptance in a group is incredibly important when it serves as a protection from exclusion, gossip, back-stabbing, verbal and physical bullying, and other types of harassment. Boys, on the other hand, obtain a certain amount of protection and acceptance through athletic and physical abilities.

> **Students who display bullying behaviors may be of a higher social standing, more assertive or verbally astute, have a powerful personality, and/or have a quick wit or tongue, helping them to easily ridicule or humiliate others.**

Educational Bullying

Educational bullying is different from the other kinds of bullying discussed because adults rather than students carry it out. *Educational bullying is when adults who perform as members of the school staff in some function use their power to either intentionally or unintentionally harm students, causing them distress.* We do not normally think of teachers, administrators, and other school staff as exhibiting bullying behaviors, but the regrettable truth is that it does occur. Most teachers do not intentionally participate in educational bullying.

A common type of educational bullying experienced by many students is the use of sarcasm in the classroom. Too many teachers use sarcasm to be humorous or as a way of controlling the classroom. This is control based on fear, students' fear of being targeted and humiliated in front of their peers. This is particularly disturbing to middle and high school students whose greatest fear is not being accepted by their peers. Sarcasm usually backfires because the degree to which an adolescent will go to save face in front of his or her peers is unparalleled!

Sarcasm and other types of educational bullying create a hostile classroom environment and, in essence, the teacher is modeling inappropriate behaviors to the students, increasing the likelihood that students will exhibit those same behaviors with their peers and teachers. "The use of sarcasm and subtle forms of ridicule by teachers is not uncommon and can contribute substantially to classroom bullying" (Rigby, 1996, p. 84).

Children with AS are more likely to experience educational bullying because of the innate characteristics of their disability. Teachers as well as students often find children with AS to be "high-maintenance" and misunderstand and/or resent some of their behaviors. It is critical that we increase our awareness of this type of bullying because it can have a very devastating effect on a child's opportunity to have positive experiences at school. Besides, it impairs a child's ability to feel safe and protected in the school environment.

Jake's Story

The following is an example of educational bullying related to a child with AS trying to report bullying.

> Jake is a fifth grader in public school who is diagnosed with AS and obsessive-compulsive disorder. He has been sitting next to Shing, a very popular boy, who teases him every day. Shing wants to make sure that all of his friends know he does not like this "uncool" boy, so he also encourages his friends to tease Jake. Jake has tried different things to make Shing stop his teasing but at the same time he really wants to be friends with Shing and the other boys. Finally, Jake cannot take it any more. He goes up to his teacher during class and asks if he can move to another seat because Shing is teasing him so badly. The teacher is surprised and responds by saying, "Shing wouldn't do that." Jake returns to his seat next to Shing, who continues to tease him all through fifth grade and into middle school.

Sometimes children who bully are popular with both teachers and peers. They may be good students who are a pleasure to have in class but covertly tease other students. By comparison, students diagnosed with AS are not always the best students and many times display disruptive or uncooperative behaviors. It is critical that teachers take all reports of bullying seriously. When they do not, it implies acceptance of bullying behavior and is an abuse of power and trust.

See Table 2.1 for a summary of the different types of bullying.

TABLE 2.1
Types of Bullying

Physical Bullying	Includes hitting, pushing, tripping, kicking, spitting on someone, pulling hair, shouldering, grabbing clothes, belongings or parts of a person's body, and any other types of hands-on physical actions.
Verbal Bullying	Includes teasing and making fun of someone, verbal threats, name-calling, and other types of incidents involving language. Some verbal bullying includes obscene gestures, eye rolling, threatening stares, or other types of nonverbal communication because it is a representation of words.
Social Bullying	Occurs when the intent is to isolate or exclude someone from peers by spreading rumors, peer shunning, humiliation, or other methods of damaging or manipulating relationships.
Educational Bullying	Occurs when adults who perform as members of the school team use their power to either intentionally or unintentionally harm students causing them distress.
	May include the use of sarcasm, being overly critical and controlling, humiliating students in front of their peers, favoring students, and being overly punitive.

A Team Approach to Bullying Prevention

The diagnosis of AS is relatively new (1994), and educators and others in our schools are still learning to recognize and capitalize on the strengths and challenges children with AS present in the classroom. Not surprisingly, there is only a beginning awareness of the vulnerability of students with AS related to bullying and social isolation.

Many parents of children with AS become quite knowledgeable about what it means to have a diagnosis of Asperger Syndrome, based on dealing with their child with AS and lots of reading, attending conferences, support groups, and so on. Parents also have a lifetime of experience with their child in a variety of social settings. When parents feel that the school staff does not value their knowledge and experience, they sometimes feel "bullied" themselves when trying to advocate for their child. This promotes feelings of anger and helplessness and an "us" versus "them" mentality instead of a team approach. Ultimately, an adversarial relationship can result, which is never in the best interest of the student.

At the same time, school staff can also feel "bullied," when they sense that parents are not open to hearing their opinions and immediately assume the worst about their intentions. For instance, if parents assume their child's teacher is deliberately ignoring bullying in the classroom when it occurs, they will probably meet with hurt feelings, anger, and/or defensiveness when talking to the teacher. The teacher may focus on defending his or her actions instead of increasing awareness and understanding of bullying in the classroom and developing strategies for taking immediate actions when bullying occurs.

School staff cannot expect to receive the support and trust of parents and students if they are not willing to mirror trust and support back. In order for the student's best interest to be served, a team approach based on mutual respect is essential so successes, concerns, and ideas can be shared between all members of the team.

In Chapter 3, I will continue to explore bullying by examining the characteristics of children who bully, the dynamics of group bullying, factors that contribute to bullying, and the consequences of being a bully.

CHAPTER 3

Children Who Bully

Julie's Story

The following example of social bullying happened to a 15-year-old girl diagnosed with AS in a private high school:

Julie came home from band practice to find her mother and father crying in the family room. They immediately asked her to sit with them and begged her to confide in them about her problem. Seeing that Julie had no idea what was going on, her parents played a voice message that had been left on their answering machine by a girl from Julie's school. The message said, "Julie, I heard about your test results, and I'm so sorry. Now I understand why you have been so tired and sick at your stomach in the morning. Let me know when you decide what you are going to do about the baby. You know I will be there for you. Call me."

Julie's parents were beside themselves assuming from the message on the answering machine that their daughter was pregnant. But that was far from the case – Julie had never been sexually active. In reality, the girl who had left the message was mad at Julie because her boyfriend had reprimanded her for making fun of Julie two days earlier. The message was a setup to get Julie in trouble, upset Julie and her family, and provide "payback." Julie convinced her parents that none of the statements were true, but even so everyone was understandably upset for a while thereafter. Julie had no idea why she had been targeted.

This particularly cruel and disturbing type of bullying requires adult intervention, including parent involvement. Even though this incident did not occur in school, it is reflective of other types of social bullying happening within the school walls. Since bullying typically involves repeated negative actions, it is important to look beyond an isolated incident and determine if other bullying has taken place.

In this chapter we will explore characteristics of children who bully, why they bully, what factors contribute to bullying behaviors, and the potential consequences of bullying.

Characteristics of Bullies

Throughout the bullying research, experts agree on certain characteristics found in children who bully. In fact, when asked to rate characteristics in identifying bullies and targets, a worldwide group of experts strongly agreed on 19 characteristics of bullies. Some of these characteristics are similar to those seen in adults who exhibit abusive behaviors. Table 3.1 provides a list of these 19 characteristics (Hazler, Carney, Green, Powell, & Jolly, 1997).

Most notable in this list are the characteristics related to power and aggression. Bullying and bullies are characterized by the use of power and aggression. Bullies are more aggressive towards their peers. They tend to have a more accepting attitude toward violence and the use of violent means to get what they want. They may also be aggressive toward adults, but are sometimes quite skilled at hiding their bullying behaviors from adult authorities in school and in the community, including their parents (Olweus, 1993). It is important that adults realize that some children who bully may be falling under their radar because they do not fit their stereotypical views of what a bully "looks like."

TABLE 3.1
19 General Characteristics of Bullies

---

1. Inappropriately perceive hostile intent in the actions of others
2. Have often been exposed to models of aggressive behaviors
3. Chronically repeat aggressive behaviors
4. Tend to have little empathy for their targets
5. Control others through verbal and physical threats
6. Quick to anger and more apt to use force
7. Angry and revengeful
8. Parents are poor social role models
9. Parents are poor role models for problem solving
10. More likely to have contact with aggressive groups
11. View aggression as the way to preserve their self-image
12. Inconsistent discipline at home
13. Focus on angry thoughts
14. Perceive physical image is important to their sense of power and control
15. Have more family problems
16. Lack of parental supervision
17. More likely to suffer physical and emotional abuse at home
18. Exhibit obsessive or rigid actions
19. Frustrate peers and create resentment

From Hazler, R.J., Carney, J.V., Green, S., Powel, R., & Jolly, L. S. (1997). Areas of expert agreement on identification of school bullies and victims. *School Psychology International, 18*(1), 5-14. Reprinted with permission.

Children who bully tend to be physically stronger than other students (especially their targets) and are physically effective in play, sports, and fights (especially boys). They desire to dominate others and assert themselves through aggression or threats of aggression. Bullies have a tendency to brag and demand their way. Children who bully may be described as hot-tempered, impulsive, easily frustrated, oppositional, defiant, and good at talking themselves out of difficult situations.

Those who bully tend to show little empathy for those they target, and are not typically anxious or insecure, having average to better than average self-esteem. They may also be average to above average in popularity and academic performance, although popularity and performance tend to wane when they get into middle school and even more so in high school (Olweus, 1993; Schwartz, 2000).

Those who bully tend to show little empathy for those they target, and are not typically anxious or insecure, having average to better than average self-esteem.

This decrease in popularity may be related to the changing dynamics of relationships with members of the opposite sex and consequent disapproval of bullying behaviors. Further, some adolescents change or hide their bullying behaviors in an effort to avoid rejection in romantic relationships. Others unfortunately continue their bullying behavior, now often exhibited through sexual harassment and date violence. As discussed in Chapter 1, it is important to recognize how bullying behaviors may develop as children mature into adolescents and young adults.

Aggressive Reaction Pattern

Typical bullies can be portrayed as having an "aggressive reaction pattern combined (in the case of boys) with physical strength" (Olweus, 1993, p. 35). This means that kids who bully want and need to feel powerful and to dominate others. They have tried out bullying and learned that it can be a very commanding tool. What they do is different than a friendly tease or a one-time statement. Instead, they develop a pattern of using their words or physical presence and abilities to physically and/or psychologically intimidate others.

For example, a physically large boy in the fourth grade typically intimidates others into letting him go out of turn on the playground equipment. Everyone has learned that if he asks for the ball or demands the court, you better just give him what he wants. He usually has a few friends with him who "have his back." If you take him on, you take them all on. He is more than ready to "back up" any threats he makes to get what he wants, and most of the other kids have given up trying to challenge him.

Historically, most of the research on bullying has focused on the more physically aggressive bullying of boys. In recent years, however, there has been a focus on aggression in girls, and we are discovering that girls can be just as aggressive as boys, only in different ways.

Girls wage social war through exclusion, peer shunning, and battles with other girls meant to damage or ruin relationships and reputations. In this age of easy access to electronic technology, the battles not only take the form of looks and words, but also include instant messaging on the Internet, emails, conference phone calls, text messages on cell phones and pagers, and nasty messages left on cell phones and answering machines. Rumors can spread like wildfire through group emails and literally change a girl's reputation over night. *Relational aggression* is the current buzzword for this type of social bullying (Wiseman, 2002). Julie's story at the beginning of this chapter is an example of this type of social bullying.

Passive Bullies

In some instances of bullying, peer onlookers observe and encourage bullying but are not as actively involved as the bully. They typically do not initiate bullying but are more or less "hanging out" with children who bully others. These somewhat less active participants are called passive bullies or followers and can be strongly influenced by witnessing bullying behaviors because they admire the bully as being powerful and having positive social status.

Passive bullies tend to be less secure and dependent (not as aggressive) and wish that they were able to assert themselves in a similar manner. In short, they are "bully wannabes." The presence of passive bullies reinforces bullying behavior. The bully feels a sense of support and acceptance and is encouraged to continue his behaviors. The mere presence of the passive bullies increases the likelihood that the bully will be successful in his encounters. The passive bullies are also likely to become increasingly more involved in bullying activities themselves and may begin to initiate bullying, taking a more active role (Olweus, 1993).

Group Bullying

In some incidents of bullying, a group mentality seems to take over so that an entire group of children participates in bullying behaviors, including passive bullies and children who are not typically involved in bullying incidents. Olweus (1993) calls this group behavior "social contagion" (p. 44). Another term for this behavior is "risky shift," described as the tendency of children and adolescents to make riskier decisions as a group than they would individually because each person feels a decreased sense of personal responsibility (Thompson, Grace, & Cohen, 2001).

This is a powerful and important dynamic because research has shown that peers are almost always present when bullying occurs (O'Connel et al., 1999). If group bullying of a particular student occurs over time, the group begins to see the target in such a diminished way that they take on the attitude that the student deserves to be bullied; that is, as someone who is "asking for it" (Olweus, 1993). This type of belief system feeds into the already impaired sense of empathy and guilt in children who bully.

If the target is a boy, other boys often feel disdain because they believe the targeted boy is not being assertive enough in defending himself; he is not being "macho" enough. For instance, if the target cries easily when bullied, other boys will consider this "sissy" behavior.

Regardless of the target's gender, students often think that the targeted student intentionally provokes others with irritating habits or personal characteristics. The reputation of the target can become so tarnished by this habitual bullying that the other students no longer apply the same social standards and rules to this student. The students become fearful that they too may become targets for ridicule and bullying simply by association with the target. Therefore, they avoid social contact and do not offer any assistance to the targeted child. This sometimes happens to a child with AS who becomes the scapegoat of a class or an entire grade. The following is a typical example of how socially rejected and isolated children with AS can become in school and other activities with their peers.

> Zack is a 16-year-old with AS. He is often bullied and doesn't have any friends at school. He desperately wants to belong and have friends, but whenever he tries to join a group at lunch or strike up a conversation with someone in class, they move away, say something mean, or ignore him. During soccer practice,

Zack follows other students around the sidelines and continues to try and talk to them when they walk away. He keeps going back to students even when they say mean things to him. For example, one day he asks Mario if he wants to come to his house after practice. When Mario responds by saying, "Shut up, freak," and walks away, Zack follows him and keeps saying, "Why not" and "What's the matter." The other kids begin to laugh at them and tease Mario by saying, "Who's your new best friend?" Mario gets embarrassed and ends up pushing Zack out of his way. When the coach finally notices, Mario tells him that Zack won't stop bothering him. The coach tells Zack he has to stand by him for the rest of practice. He cautions Mario not to get physical and tells him to get back to the practice drill.

As illustrated below, sometimes children who are bullied respond by starting to bully others. Many times they are just trying to put on a tougher persona so they will be left alone. Some children who bully are victims at home.

Children Who Are Both Bully and Target

Some students take on the role of both bully and victim. These students are typically the most rejected by their peers and need an incredible amount of support and intervention. It is unclear whether the targets become bullies to retaliate against how they have been treated; that is, if they just feel it is their turn to be the bully and begin to treat others the way they have been treated (Forero, McLellan, Rissel, & Bauman, 1999; Swearer, Song, Cary, Eagle, & Mickelson, 2001). We will discuss this high-risk group in more detail in Chapter 4 when we look more closely at targets of bullying.

The following describes a student who begins to bully others as a result of being a frequent target of bullying.

Taro is 10 years old and diagnosed with AS. He has been bullied in school every year, but the fourth grade has been his worst year ever. He used to think that everyone who talked to him was his friend, but now he realizes that he doesn't have friends and that a lot of kids are mean to him at school. He is angry about the way he is being treated and wants it to stop. When he sees someone else being bullied, he often joins in because he is glad he is not the one being teased.

Taro's behavior brings us to the reasons why children bully others. There are many reasons, but the common themes continue to be associated with power and aggression.

Why Children Bully

A pattern develops when looking for potential motives or psychological reasons behind bullying behaviors. Certainly, power, dominance, and a desire to be in control and subdue others are major parts of the dynamics. Children who bully seem to have developed a level of hostility or negative feelings toward their environment that causes them to derive a sense of pleasure or satisfaction from inflicting suffering and unpleasantness on others – a sort of a "misery loves company" type of thinking. Also, bullies often coerce favors or things of value from their victims. Finally, many bullies unfortunately gain a certain amount of prestige among their peers – an elevation of their social status based on their ability to be strong and in control (Olweus, 1993).

What Contributes to the Development of Bullying Behaviors?

Considerable discussion and thought have been given to the possible antecedents or factors that impact whether a child develops bullying behaviors. Most of the research has focused on what type of parenting practices or home environments might produce children who bully. Is there a specific type of parenting style that promotes this type of aggression in children?

Factors That Promote/Contribute to Bullying

Four factors seem to have the most impact or importance related to bullying. These include parental practices and attitudes related to aggression and power, as well as the child's temperament. Olweus summarizes these parenting practices that contribute to bullying as "too little love and care and too much 'freedom' in childhood" (Olweus, 1993, p. 39). Table 3.2 summarizes these family factors.

Finally, schools can promote and reinforce bullying by allowing bullying behaviors to go unchallenged. When adults give mixed messages about what is acceptable social behavior, they inadvertently promote a community where bullying is tolerated and becomes pervasive.

TABLE 3.2
Family Factors That Promote Bullying

- A negative attitude toward the child from his or her caretakers, especially mothers, in conjunction with a lack of warmth and involvement seems to increase the risk that the child will become aggressive and lack empathy for others

- The primary caretakers' permissive tolerance of a higher level of aggressive behavior in their child and siblings

- The use of child-rearing methods that focus on asserting power through means of physical punishment and violent, overemotional outbursts

- The child's temperament; if the child tends to be more active and easily angered or frustrated, he or she may be more likely to develop aggressive tendencies

---

Adapted from Olweus, D. (1993). *Bullying at school: What we know and what we can do.* Oxford: Blackwell Publishers, pp. 39-40.

Consequences for Bullies

Targets are not the only ones for whom bullying has consequences. There are also consequences for the bullies. Bullies are more likely to be involved in other negative behaviors such as smoking, drinking, juvenile delinquency, gang membership, fighting, and drugs (Nansel et al., 2001). Further, a significant relationship has been noted between bullying and higher levels of depression for boys and girls. Also, students who bully are more likely to dislike school.

As stated earlier, some children are both bully and victim. These children are significantly more depressed and anxious than typical children or children who "only" bully. Since they suffer the effects of being both bully and target, they experience the most significant negative consequences, both socially and psychologically. The consequences for both bullies and targets can be severe and highlight the need for early intervention.

The topics discussed in this chapter help us understand the typical characteristics of children who bully, factors that promote bullying, and the motivation behind bullying. This information will help direct our efforts in determining appropriate strategies and programs for bullying prevention.

The next chapter will look at similar topics, this time related to children who are typically targeted for bullying. Specifically, I will discuss characteristics of targets, profiling, how children respond to bullying, what contributes to children becoming targets, and the consequences of being bullied.

CHAPTER 4

Typical Children Targeted for Bullying

Jose's Story

The following is a description of a boy in elementary school who is frequently the target of bullying. Jose is a typical *passive* target.

Jose is alone most of the time. He likes to read at lunch, isn't good at sports, and is physically smaller than a lot of boys in his class. He tried several sports activities, but was usually the worst player on the team and tended not to be aggressive enough to please his teammates. The other boys on the team usually got frustrated with him and complained to the coach when he was played the amount of time required for each player. Now that Jose is 11, the teams are even more competitive, and he is well aware that no one wants him on their team. He doesn't play on any sports teams, but still gets harassed by the other boys when they play team sports in physical education class. Sometimes the students beg the P.E. teacher to let them pick teams and when this is allowed, Jose is always the last pick. It is humiliating for him. Some of the boys have started calling him "gay boy" in the halls, at recess, and during class when the teacher is not around. Jose usually gets very upset when this happens, and it seems as if more and more boys are teasing him.

Trevor's Story

The following description is of a boy in elementary school who is also a frequent target of bullying. Trevor is characterized as a *provocative* target.

Trevor likes to be around other boys his age although he typically gets along better with boys who are younger than him. He likes to play soccer and brags about how well he can play. In truth, he is probably one of the worst players on the team. He is always begging the coach to put him in and gets mad if any of the other boys on the team say anything negative about his playing. He often gets in trouble in class because he doesn't stay on task and talks excessively trying to socialize. He doesn't have any close friends and is frequently bullied. Whenever Trevor is teased, he gets agitated and tries to tease back but the other boys take up for each other and just laugh at him. A couple of neighborhood kids play with him after school, but they won't have anything to do with him when they are at school. Another student in Trevor's class is in special education, and he gets teased a lot like Trevor. Sometimes Trevor joins in and teases him too. The other kids typically tell on Trevor whenever they get the chance. However, when it comes to their friends, they consider telling on their friends "ratting" and not cool.

This chapter will look at the characteristics of children typically targeted for bullying (both passive and provocative targets), profiling, how children respond to bullying, what factors contribute to becoming a target, and the consequences of being a target.

Characteristics of Targets

The general characteristics of targets have been well documented through research. They typically fall into two groups: the majority are passive or nonaggressive targets, with a smaller group labeled as provocative or aggressive targets.

Passive Targets

Passive targets tend to be physically weaker than their peers (especially boys) and may have body anxiety (afraid of being hurt or hurting themselves, physically ineffective in play, sports, and fights, and lack physical coordination). They tend to be more cautious, quiet, withdrawn, and passive and prone to emotional outbursts when upset. They are described as being anxious, insecure, having poor self-esteem, and are typically viewed by others as "easy targets."

These children tend to have difficulty asserting themselves in groups physically and verbally and are usually not aggressive and do not tease. They often relate better to adults than same-age peers. While their academic performance may be poor to good in the earlier grades, their performance usually worsens in middle school (Olweus, 1993; Schwartz, 2000).

Jose's story describes a typical passive target. It is not surprising that the primary form of harassment is directed toward Jose's masculinity or gender status. This is a common type of harassment with boys starting in elementary and continuing through high school. At an age when boys are trying to figure out how to be men, they tend to have a narrow view of what constitutes acceptable masculine behaviors, leading to a disturbing trend in schools and elsewhere for boys to monitor and question each other's sexuality. This type of "heterosexual policing" includes a considerable amount of what can be described at a minimum as homophobic behavior and, in its worst form, as sexual harassment. In some instances, the targeted boy's reputation is irreparably damaged in the eyes of his peers. The type of drama it creates may be compared to a girl being labeled a "dyke" or the "class slut."

In middle school especially, there is little tolerance for differences, and most children are desperately trying not to stand out from their peers in any way that might be perceived as negative or odd. If the target of this type of bullying is in fact homosexual, the damage is even more brutal because it attacks the child's self-concept and self-esteem at a very vulnerable time in his or her development.

Middle school is a time when students are developing emotionally, cognitively, sexually, and physically in ways that they can barely keep up with. It is a time when there is little acceptance and tolerance for anything or anyone that varies from stereotypical norms related to masculinity and femininity. Not being accepted by your peers is devastating, especially during this critical time when peer acceptance is so important. Bullying tends to increase during the middle school years and those who are bullied often experience a drop in their grades. It seems that so much energy is directed toward "fitting in" along with the added stress of dealing with bullying that these targeted students are not able to adequately deal with learning in school. That is, without safety and security, love and belonging, there is no learning.

> *It seems that so much energy is directed toward "fitting in" along with the added stress of dealing with bullying that these targeted students are not able to adequately deal with learning in school.*

For reasons just discussed, typical insults used against boys are variations of "girl, sissy, fag, baby, crybaby, mama's boy, nerd, retard, spaz, fatty, and shrimp." Boys are expected to be "physically competent, aggressive, stoic, and independent" (Thompson et al., 2001, p. 173). Since the typical characteristics of passive targets tend to go against these general stereotypes, they create opportunities for peer harassment.

Girls are scrutinized by a similar type of policing, based on narrow views of how girls are supposed to behave and look. These views are also based on general social stereotypes. Typical insults aimed at girls are different versions of supposed failures at being social or attractive such as, "stuck-up, bitchy, flat-chested, fatty, ugly, and slut" (Thompson et al., 2001, p. 173).

Boys are required to be strong, athletic, and masculine. They aren't supposed to be emotional and need to be "tough" to be accepted. Girls, on the other hand, are supposed to be physically attractive and "nice girls." They are not supposed to be confrontational or show aggression, and their acceptance is based primarily on looks, clothes, and "being nice." These stereotypes affect both passive and provocative targets.

Provocative Targets

Provocative or aggressive targets may show a combination of anxious and aggressive reaction patterns. Provocative targets also may be physically weaker and have body anxiety. They tend to have a negative view of themselves, are unhappy, anxious, and insecure. Provocative targets may include an increased representation of boys with certain exceptionalities such as attention deficit disorder, oppositional defiant disorder, AS, and other disabilities whereby children tend to exhibit traits such as anxiety and impulsivity. Provocative targets are typically boys, possibly due to the social pressures girls experience related to inhibiting aggression and avoiding direct confrontation.

Provocative targets may try to bully weaker students, particularly someone of a lower social standing. They often attempt to talk back or fight when bullied but are not very effective at it. They may be hyperactive, hot-tempered, restless, and lacking in focus. They are also typically viewed as offensive, rude, high-maintenance, clumsy, and immature with irritating habits.

Provocative targets are highly disliked by their peers, and even some adults, including teachers, view them with disdain. As a result, many students, sometimes an entire class, may be involved in bullying these children. Trevor's story is an example of a child who is a provocative target. Because his behaviors annoy his teachers and are disruptive, he is thought of as a troublemaker. The teachers do not typically see the teasing and bullying behaviors of the other kids because they are more covert. Trevor doesn't understand why he has trouble making friends. Without intervention, provocative targets like Trevor are at extremely high risk for lifelong difficulties such as depression and decreased self-esteem (Olweus, 1993; Schwartz, 2000).

A group of experts strongly agree on 21 characteristics of targets. Table 4.1 provides a list of these characteristics (Hazler et al., 1997).

Profiling

Because of recent violent events in our schools, there is considerable interest in identifying potentially troubled students. Some authorities have recommended using warning lists, checklists, teacher screening, and/or other means of profiling as a way of identifying the characteristics of children who are potentially high risk before school violence happens. These are all similar ways of "profiling," or matching children to the characteristics of students who have in the past committed random acts of violence in school (Bender, Shubert, & McLaughlin, 2001).

TABLE 4.1
21 General Characteristics of a Target

---

1. Have ineffective social skills
2. Have poor interpersonal skills
3. Believe that they cannot control their environment
4. Have underlying fears of personal inadequacy
5. Socially isolated
6. Afraid of going to school
7. Physically younger, smaller, and weaker than peers
8. Poor self-concept
9. Have difficulty relating to peers
10. Less popular
11. Blame themselves for their problems
12. Given labels suggesting inadequacy
13. Limited skills for gaining acceptance and success
14. Limited communication skills under stress
15. Have physical mannerisms associated with depression
16. Have frequent feelings of personal inadequacy
17. Perform self-destructive actions
18. Believe others are more capable of handling things
19. Feel external factors have a greater impact than internal control
20. Have family members over-involved in their decisions and activities
21. Perceived progressive failures cause this person to put forth less effort with each presenting opportunity

---

From Hazler, R.J., Carney, J.V., Green, S., Powel, R., & Jolly, L. S. (1997). Areas of expert agreement on identification of school bullies and victims. *School Psychology International, 18*(1), 5-14. Reprinted by permission.

Based on the results of a study conducted by the United States Secret Service on 41 school shooters involved in 37 attacks since 1974, it was concluded that profiling is probably a waste of time and that resources would be better used on prevention. The results did, however, point out that many attackers (at least two-thirds) felt bullied and persecuted before the attack:

> Bullying was not a factor in every case, and clearly not every child who is bullied in school will pose a risk for targeted violence in school. Nevertheless, in a number of the incidents of targeted school violence studied, attackers described being bullied in terms that suggested that these experiences approached torment. These attackers told of behaviors that, if they occurred in the workplace, likely would meet legal definitions of harassment and/or assault. (Vossekuil, Fein, Reddy, Borum, & Modzeleski, 2002, p. 38)

These findings emphasize the importance of continuing to shed light on bullying in our schools and making bullying prevention programs a priority in an effort to provide a safer environment for our children.

Implications for Children with AS

The characteristics of many children with special needs, and in particular children with AS, place them at significant risk of being identified as "troubled students" even though they are typically targets of bullying. As we discuss the characteristics of children diagnosed with AS related to bullying in Chapter 5, it will become clear that children with AS exhibit many of the same characteristics or behaviors as passive and provocative targets. Consequently, we need to make sure that being labeled as "troubled kids" or "potential time bombs" due to characteristics innate to their disability does not further harm children with special needs by helping to prevent them from becoming the targets for bullying and violence.

Behavioral Responses of Children Who Are Targeted

Children who are targets of bullying usually aggravate any behavioral differences they already have by acting overly needy or desperate to their peers. Targets tend to go back to the peers who reject them, making unsuccessful attempts to interact socially. These children are also noted to have poor social skills, making these attempts even more awkward (Troy & Sroufe, 1987).

Passive targets rarely fight back when hurt, instead trying to continue the relationship. Provocative targets follow much the same pattern of trying to continue the relationship with their abusers. However, they exhibit more behaviors that result in provoking incidents. Children targeted for bullying long to be accepted by their peers and tend to return over and over to peers who have abused them. Trying to find a reason for such seemingly illogical behavior, Troy and Sroufe (1987) noted that targets of peers usually experienced inconsistent responses from their primary caregivers varying from responsiveness to rejection. This created a tendency for these children to be more accepting of rejection and to take the role of victim in other relationships as well.

It is possible that children with AS demonstrate similar responses to being rejected by their peers because they are unable to effectively process the social responses of other students. In other words, they desire a relationship but are unable to use past experiences to accurately predict whether they will be accepted or rejected by their peers.

If these patterns continue into adulthood, there is reason to be concerned that these characteristics may create risk for further victimization as they parallel relationships seen in domestic abuse. That is, many victims of domestic abuse stay in a relationship with the abuser and seem unable more than unwilling to disconnect from the abusive relationship.

Stabilization of Target Status

Victimization appears to be fairly stable over time. Thus, Olweus (1993) found that the same children tend to be targeted again and again. Even if the targets change classes and interact with different peers, they are typically found and targeted by other students who bully and can be identified as a target by peers and teachers. This also seems to hold true for children who bully. That is, children who bully tend to continue being involved in bullying activities over time. The impact of these findings highlights even more the importance of intervention and prevention. In short, without intervention bully-target problems will most likely continue (Olweus, 1993).

Victimization appears to be fairly stable over time . . . This also seems to hold true for children who bully.

Stabilization of target status seems to be particularly true for children with AS, according to anecdotal reports from parents and professionals. For example, Ling is an 8-year-old diagnosed with AS.

She experienced severe and frequent bullying in first and second grade, so her parents decided to place her in a small, private school for third grade. Before long, Ling started to have many of the same types of bullying experiences. Initially, the other girls in the class made attempts at including Ling, but soon she was being excluded at lunch and recess. She would have the occasional girl over to her house, but the invitations were never reciprocated. Some of the girls started teasing her about asking so many questions during class and began calling her "clueless." Ling's parents concluded that whatever made Ling a target for bullying and exclusion couldn't be fixed by moving her to a different school or class and began talking to the school about how they could work together on bullying prevention that would benefit all the students.

What Contributes to Becoming a Target?

More research has been directed at identifying contributing factors to the development of bullying behaviors than at discovering how environmental and parenting factors might influence or contribute to a child becoming a target. However, we do know that parents of children who are targets tend to be overprotective and over-involved in the decisions and activities of their children. This may effectively make children more dependent and fearful, which are characteristics that are typically seen in children who are targeted for bullying. There is nothing to indicate that typical passive targets lack love or attention from their parents. Quite the opposite, targets were noted to be particularly close and had more positive relationships to their parents (especially their mothers) than to their peers in general (especially boys). Based on these findings, Olweus (1993) suggested that to decrease the likelihood that anxious, insecure children develop into targets, it is important to promote independence, self-confidence, and assertiveness.

Consequences of Being Targeted for Bullying

Short-term outcomes associated with being the target of bullying include anxiety, physical and psychological distress, lack of focus in school, and refusal to go to school. In the long term, depression, suicide, withdrawn behaviors, aggression, and physical health problems (headaches, stomach problems) may also occur.

Furthermore, consequences in adulthood can be serious as well. Targets of bullying are at a much higher risk for depression and a negative view of themselves even as they reach adulthood. The severity of the abuse or victimization is highly correlated with the level of adult depression. This seems to occur regardless of whether there is continued harassment into adulthood (Olweus, 1993; Pepler & Craig, 2000).

It may be that former targets internalize the negative feedback they received from their peers and, therefore, continue to suffer from low self-esteem and often depression. As would be expected, children who are both bully and target appear to suffer the most negative consequences. As noted, these children are also typically the most rejected by their peers (Olweus, 1993). They are more likely to be provocative targets that irritate peers and adults and respond to the rejection and bullying by bullying others in return. Finally, there is a group of children who are targets at home and bullies at school, modeling the behavior of their siblings and/or the adults in their family.

School is where most bullying occurs. Insights into the characteristics of both bullies and targets empower adults in authority to take steps toward making positive changes in the school community. All children are capable of taking on the role of both bully and target, and some do. It is the role of adults to model prosocial behaviors and teach children how to interact with each other in caring, tolerant ways.

The next chapter examines how bullying affects children with AS. I will explore the characteristics of children with AS, drawing comparisons to characteristics of children who are typically bullied. This will include a discussion of their social challenges related to bullying, with a focus on language and predicting peer behaviors. Other factors that can contribute to being targeted for bullying and consequences of chronic victimization will be addressed as well.

CHAPTER 5

Perfect Targets:
Children with Asperger Syndrome

Nick's Story

The following incident involves a 13-year-old boy diagnosed with Asperger Syndrome (AS) who was attending seventh grade in a public middle school.

Today Nick has a substitute in band class. Usually when there is a substitute in band, the students clown around and talk more than usual. There is little else provided for the students to do, unless they bring work from another class. Nick is looking forward to socializing and wastes no time talking to the students seated near him. When the teacher tells Nick to quit talking, he says something back that the teacher perceives as extremely rude. (Later, Nick cannot remember what he said, but he does not remember it as being rude.) The substitute takes Nick out in the hall and says, "What the Hell is the matter with you?"

When Nick tells his mother what happened after he gets home, she asks how it made him feel. Nick replies, "Every day I wonder what is wrong with me. I don't need a teacher cursing and yelling in my face telling me something is wrong with me!"

Although Nick's experience portrays an extreme example of educational bullying by a substitute teacher unfamiliar with the students in the class, many children with AS receive more subtle, but still negative, types of feedback almost every day. For example, they are constantly reminded of how they are not "fitting in" or "measuring up" academically, behaviorally, and socially. In this instance, Nick reported the incident to the vice principal, and the teacher's actions were reported to the district office, resulting in the substitute not being allowed to substitute at Nick's school any more. He continued to substitute at other schools in the district, however.

This chapter explores bullying related to children with AS. This will include the characteristics of these children and how they compare to typical targets of bullying, the social challenges of children with AS related to bullying, and other factors that contribute to being targeted. Finally, the consequences of chronic victimization will be considered as well.

Characteristics of Children with AS

As mentioned, the characteristics of children with AS place them at significant risk for bullying. According to available research (Little, 2002) and anecdotal information, children with AS are almost without exception targets of bullying. In reviewing the characteristics of passive and provocative targets, it becomes clear that they share many similarities with children with AS. Consequently, the innate characteristics related to the social-communication concerns of their disorder make children with AS perfect targets.

Children with AS usually present as either more introverted or more extroverted. The more introverted students tend to spend a lot of time alone and be fairly passive about seeking out social contact with others. For example, Jamal is 8 years old and diagnosed with AS. He tends to finish his work quickly and then spends his free time reading and looking at maps. He doesn't initiate many conversations with his classmates unless he is talking about his favorite subject, maps. He usually spends recess walking around the perimeter of the playground counting his steps.

The more extroverted students with AS tend to more actively pursue others and initiate social interactions with their classmates. Aiko, an 11-year-old with AS, seeks out social interactions with her classmates but does so in socially awkward ways. She monologues about her area of interest, Japanese animation, is inflexible, and has difficulty cooperating and taking turns when in a group.

Howlin (2002) uses the terms *avoidant/passive* (introverted) and *engaging* (extroverted) to describe these two types of social presentations, observing that children with either social presentation tend to frustrate and be rejected by their peers.

Avoidant/Passive

Children with an avoidant/passive pattern of behavior often isolate themselves, preferring objects and special interests to playmates. When they do play, a lack of reciprocity (give and take) is evident. Because these children tend to be loners and do not involve themselves in many of the interactions of interest to their peers, they are more noticed by teachers, parents, and other professionals, such as Jamal in the example above. Professionals may identify children who present as avoidant/ passive earlier because their social differences are more obviously out of the norm (Howlin, 2002).

Engaging

When demonstrating an engaging pattern, children often exhibit excessive bossiness, inflexibility, and difficulty with social interactions during play. Children who present with this more active and engaging pattern may not be identified as early by professionals and are sometimes thought of as simply odd and ill-mannered (Howlin, 2002).

Because these children tend to have irritating habits and can be demanding and seemingly oblivious of the feelings of others, adults and professionals tend to view them as odd and focus on their inappropriate behaviors. Because of their characteristic inflexibility, they are often seen as oppositional and defiant, with behaviors ranging from sensory issues to difficulty dealing with change.

Table 5.1 summarizes typical characteristics of children diagnosed with AS. Table 5.2 and Table 5.3 show the characteristic differences seen with avoidant/passive and engaging social presentations, respectively.

TABLE 5.1
General Characteristics of
Children with Asperger Syndrome

- Frustrate peers
- Rejected by peers
- Clumsy; may be ineffective in play, sports and fights
- Difficulty engaging in age-expected social interactions
- Formal "little professor" speech
- Emotionally vulnerable; easily stressed
- Anxious
- Inflexible
- Easily fatigued; tendency to be sedentary
- Socially naïve
- Viewed as "easy targets"

Adapted from Howlin, R. (2002). *Understanding Asperger Syndrome (social dyslexia).*
Retrieved January 29, 2002, from http://www.aspergersmichigan.com/asperger.html.

TABLE 5.2
Avoidant/Passive Social Presentation

- Are passive/withdrawn socially
- Tend to be "loners"
- Prefer objects and special interests (sometimes instead of playmates)
- Lack reciprocity in play
- May be identified by professionals at earlier age
- Relate better to adults than peers
- Viewed as "easy targets"

Adapted from Howlin, R. (2002). *Understanding Asperger Syndrome (social dyslexia).*
Retrieved January 29, 2002, from http://www.aspergersmichigan.com/asperger.html.

TABLE 5.3
Engaging Social Presentation

- Are most rejected by peers
- Disliked by some adults in authority, including teachers
- Have irritating habits
- Lack focus; impulsive and immature
- Attempt to fight or talk back when bullied but ineffective
- Demonstrate excessive bossiness
- Seek out social interactions in an "in your face" kind of way
- Tend to receive a diagnosis at a later age; seen as "odd" and ill-mannered
- Seen as demanding and oblivious to the feelings and responses of others

---

Adapted from Howlin, R. (2002). *Understanding Asperger Syndrome (social dyslexia)*. Retrieved January 29, 2002, from http://www.aspergersmichigan.com/asperger.html.

Parallels to the Characteristics of Bullying Targets

In a closer examination of the characteristics of children with AS compared to characteristics of children typically targeted for bullying, the commonalities become astonishing. That is, the characteristics of passive targets are similar to the avoidant/passive social presentation commonly seen in children with AS whereas the characteristics of provocative targets parallel the engaging social presentation noted in some children with AS. It is no wonder that children diagnosed with AS are targeted for bullying so often.

Social Challenges of Children with AS as They Relate to Bullying

Children with AS lack the social skills and social support to counter their attackers and, therefore, often become chronic targets of bullying. The truth is that no child has the necessary social skills to stop severe bullying without adult intervention and support. Thompson, Cohen, and Grace (2002) refer to the most at-risk children as "rejected children." Constituting 10-12% of the class, these children are the ones who are alone, either because no one wants to be friends with them or because other children are afraid to befriend them at the risk of becoming targets of teasing and bullying themselves.

These rejected children are referred to as either *rejected-submissive* or *rejected-aggressive*. The submissive group rarely puts up much of a fight when rejected, but children in the aggressive group tend to fight back against their social exclusion and rejection.

Not surprisingly, the aggressive group is more likely to eventually display bullying behaviors in response to constant harassment by their peers. However, not all children who are chronically bullied become bullies themselves. Many children suffer in silence and internalize their problems, thereby becoming anxious and even depressed. A child's particular social personality or presentation is one of many factors that determine how he or she reacts to bullying when it occurs.

Let's take a closer look at the social issues that create the most difficulty for children with AS and contribute to their vulnerability in school. Language and socialization issues and difficulty predicting the behaviors of others are key areas when considering the challenges of children diagnosed with AS.

Language and Socialization

Students with AS have language and socialization issues. Difficulties with the pragmatics of social language along with other social deficits contribute to problems fitting in with peers in social situations and being more vulnerable to bullying and teasing. Cognitive, sensory, and/or physical differences may also contribute to ineffectiveness in academic success, play activities, sports, and self-defense. Myles and Adreon (2001) identify several social deficits that commonly cause difficulties for adolescents with AS. They include:

- An inability to interpret the meaning behind nonverbal communication
- Difficulty with social conversations
- A tendency for literal interpretations
- Difficulty taking or considering another person's perspective

- Lack of understanding about the social rules that most people know about intuitively (hidden curriculum)
- Lack of awareness of how things said in one conversation can affect future interactions with that person. (pp. 15-17)

In addition, Bashe and Kirby (2001) list the following ways in which children with AS may exhibit impaired social interactions:

- May appear to lack common sense or social awareness
- May not be able to tell the difference between playful teasing without harmful intent from serious bullying
- May think in terms of black and white and apply rules rigidly without taking into consideration all pertinent factors
- May have trouble keeping appropriate physical distance during social interactions or make inappropriate physical contact without harmful intent
- May be the object of covert bullying by typical peers
- May get in trouble for an overt reaction which probably includes inappropriate behavior in response to bullying
- May feel emotionally overwrought by the strain of dealing with the social realities of daily life in school; becoming stressed and anxious, unable to predict what will happen next. (pp. 377-378)

Inability to Predict Others' Behavior

As discussed in Chapter 1, the main strategy used by students to make themselves feel safe in school is predicting the behavior of others. Children with AS are typically extremely challenged when it comes to trying to predict social situations and behaviors. This is due in part to their theory-of-mind deficits, which inhibit their ability to take the perspective of another person or predict what others may be thinking or feeling (Howlin, Baron-Cohen, & Hadwin, 1999). This places children with AS at a great disadvantage and increases their anxiety and stress levels, impairing their ability to stay safe at school and negatively impacting their school experience. Indeed, many students with AS are unable to feel safe and secure enough to move on to actual learning. This is critically important to understand because it is at the heart of understanding the world of children who live with AS.

Other Factors That Contribute to Being Targeted

When working with children diagnosed with AS, it is important to remember that because of their disability, the dynamics of personal attributes, peer relationships, and family influences may be somewhat different than those seen with other children who are targets of bullying. Clearly, personal characteristics, including physical, behavioral, and social-cognitive factors, play a significant role in whether a child with AS becomes the target of bullying. Let's look at special considerations to keep in mind when dealing with these children in terms of parenting styles, peer relationships, and reactions to bullying experiences.

Parenting Styles

In general, children who have overprotective parents (especially mothers) and are not allowed independence may be more at risk for bullying than others (Perry, Hodges, & Egan, 2001). It is suggested that this type of parenting (called "helicopter parents") does not promote responsible learning in children (Cline & Fay, 1992). This dynamic may be different for children with AS, whose parents tend to "hover" more in an effort to set their child up for successful interactions and experiences and, in many cases, to make sure their child remains safe. Thus, this is often more of a reaction to the unique challenges of their child's disability than an innate overprotective parenting style.

It is important that educators understand this dynamic so that they do not inadvertently cause parents distress by implying that they are enabling their child's behavior and by doing so are making them at risk for bullying. However, it is also vital that both parents and educators work to foster as much independence as possible without placing children with AS at greater risk for negative social and academic experiences. This is a fine line, and one that parents of children with AS have to walk every single day.

Many parents of children with AS feel that others, sometimes educators, are judging them when they ask for modifications or special considerations for their children. Considering the amount of stress parents of a child with AS often experience, particularly when their child is being bullied, critical reactions like these need to be avoided at all costs. Even more harmful is when adults and peers blame the target of bullying, the child with AS, often causing him or her to start self-blaming.

Peer Relationships

Peer relationships are greatly impacted by the personal attributes of children with AS. The degree of peer rejection, the quality of peer friendships or absence of friendships, group dynamics, and the prevailing attitudes present in the school community toward bullying behaviors all affect bully-target relationships. If a child is rejected by his peers and does not have friends, he is extremely high risk for bullying because the bully will most likely perceive little consequence for his or her behavior. In other words, the bully will not see any social risk or consequences from peers and perhaps even by the school staff. This is particularly true for provocative targets, who are usually more disliked and shunned because their behaviors are seen as irritating, overemotional, and socially inept (Perry et al., 2001).

Reactions to Bullying Experiences

Whenever children experience bullying, they try to figure out why this is happening to them, especially when the victimization is chronic. If a child decides that she is being bullied because there is something "wrong" with her or because of something she cannot change or control, she is more likely to experience anxiety, depression, and decreased self-esteem. However, if a child contributes his negative experiences to something external, such as a lack of teacher supervision or being in the wrong place at the wrong time, he experiences less anxiety and depression and does not blame himself as much (Graham & Juvonen, 2001).

Whenever children experience bullying, they try to figure out why this is happening to them, especially when the victimization is chronic.

Many times, children with AS receive feedback from their peers, teachers, and even parents, that leads them to believe that there is something wrong with the way they are behaving and/or feeling and that, therefore, there must be something innately wrong with them. This feedback may be unintentional, simply an attempt to motivate children to change their behaviors. For example, parents sometimes unintentionally, or out of anger and frustration, give feedback that makes the child feel she is unable to change her situation and/or that things would be better if she could just change who she is. Teachers need to be very mindful about harming a child's self-esteem by making negative statements in front of peers because of the already low social status of many children with AS. Also, peers can be cruel in attacking a child in a very personal way by saying things like "you're so weird," "you're a reject," "why would anyone want to be your friend," and so on. These types of behavior can be very damaging and should never be tolerated.

Next, the discussion turns to how consequences can be even more damaging to the victim if bullying and negative feedback are chronic and frequent.

Consequences of Chronic Victimization

We know that children with AS are frequent targets of bullying, but it is important to understand why children diagnosed with AS are at such a high risk of being targeted. It is also important to understand that bullying is a complex set of behaviors and that children can take on different roles depending on the circumstances.

Children with AS may exhibit many types of behaviors based on how anxious or stressed out they feel. If they have needs at school that are not being met (social, sensory, safety, or academic), they may exhibit disruptive or inappropriate behaviors and act accordingly. Increased understanding and awareness will help adults identify the function of these behaviors. If chronic harassment is allowed to continue unchallenged, any child may eventually lash out at others in response. This is exactly what we do not want to happen because it will produce children who are both target and bully and, as a result, will continue the cycle of violence and create children who are the most vulnerable to serious consequences.

Researchers have identified a small percentage of children, 5-10% of targets, who experience such severe and frequent victimization that they are high risk for serious consequences and require a tremendous amount of support in order to progress positively (Pepler & Craig, 2000). Consequences such as anxiety, school refusal, depression, and physical health problems can result when severe and/or chronic bullying is present. Depression in adulthood is also a concern.

Miguel is a 15-year-old with AS. One of his classmates (Dylan) kept challenging him to a fight after school. He finally agreed to meet Dylan after school because of the embarrassment these challenges caused him with the other students. Things didn't go well, and Miguel ended up with lots of bruises up and down both of his arms because he was unable to effectively defend himself; he never hit Dylan back. Every day after school, Dylan demanded that Miguel show everyone the bruises on his arms as proof that he "had been beaten up." Miguel denied what happened and kept saying Dylan never showed up. This made Dylan even more persistent, so he began to hit Miguel on the arm trying to make him flinch from the pain of his bruising. Miguel wouldn't dress out for gym because he knew his classmates would see his bruises. After a few days of this treatment, Miguel refused to go to school. He finally told his parents what had happened and begged them to let him stay home until the bruises healed so the other kids wouldn't know he was such a "sissy."

Children with AS usually have such low social standing and persistent experiences with bullying that they are disproportionately represented in the 5-10% who are at most risk for consequences due to bullying. The most serious negative consequences may be avoided, however, if these patterns are broken – the earlier the better.

Bullying is pervasive in our schools and has become one more aspect of the hidden curriculum, or social rules that most people understand without being taught, that children with AS struggle to understand. If typical children have such difficulty understanding how to deal with bullying, then imagine the challenge it presents to children with AS who lack the innate skills to effectively handle complex social situations. The good news is that peers can often be useful resources in helping students understand the hidden curriculum (Heinrichs, 2003).

Students who are bystanders when bullying occurs are a key component in these efforts. The next chapter discusses the role of bystanders, including characteristics of bystanders, how the school culture affects bystander roles and reactions, implications for children with AS, and the potential impact bystanders can have in bullying prevention.

CHAPTER 6

The Bystanders

Becky's Story

The following incident involves a 10-year-old girl attending fifth grade in a public elementary school.

Becky is a good student and, although she is not considered extremely popular, she gets along well with most of her peers and is not typically teased or bullied. She is not allowed to have friends over very often so she has a hard time making close friends because she only sees the other kids at school.

There is a new girl in Becky's class this year. Her name is Sarah, and she is the object of a lot of teasing. Sarah is taller and more developed than the other girls. She wears the same two dresses all the time and has problems with body odor. She also experiences frequent outbreaks of facial acne. To make matters worse, when Sarah is called on in class, she often stutters. The boys have started a rumor that she does not wear any underwear, and they frequently drop their pencils in order to get a peek up her dress. The girls avoid the bathroom stall that Sarah uses because after she leaves the stall you can smell her body odor. Becky does not get involved in teasing others and usually feels very disturbed when she observes bullying and teasing. She does not intervene but stays away and does not join in. It seems everyone has been teasing Sarah, and the entire class basically ostracizes her. No one has taken the time to get to know her.

One day during bathroom break, several girls are already in the bathroom when Becky walks into the stall that Sarah usually uses. Becky immediately walks back out of the stall saying, "I don't want to use this bathroom. This is the one Sarah uses." As she walks out of the stall, she runs right into Sarah, who is standing there with a shocked look on her face. Becky is horrified and ashamed, and immediately leaves the restroom. She never tells Sarah she is sorry, but she is truly sorry for what she has done and feels confused as to why she did it. She just did it on impulse to "fit in."

A few days later the teacher sends Sarah to the office to do a chore so she can talk to the rest of the class while Sarah is out of the room. She begins to tell the class how ashamed she is of each and every one of them for being so mean to Sarah and that because of the teasing Sarah will be transferring to another school. She warns them not to say anything else mean to Sarah and not to let on that they know about her leaving the school. The teacher also tells the students that it is too late to tell Sarah that they are sorry.

Becky was devastated. She felt certain that her hurtful comment was the "last straw" for Sarah. She wanted to say she was sorry, but the teacher made it clear that they were not to say anything to Sarah. Becky never saw Sarah after that day, but she thought about her often, even into adulthood. After Sarah left, the topic of teasing was never again mentioned in class.

This is my story. I am Becky in the story, and this happened when I was in fifth grade. The name of the target has been changed. I do think of "Sarah" often, and wonder what the rest of her school years were like. I still feel ashamed and guilty when I think of my role in her pain, and even now wish I could find her and apologize or make some kind of amends. I have shared this story with my own children in an effort to show them how their roles in bullying and teasing can affect others and their own lives.

Was I a bystander, a passive bully, a bully, or all three? Why did I choose to tease this girl when it went against my typical belief system and behavior patterns? I will try to answer some of these questions in this chapter as we explore the roles of bystanders and the dynamics and characteristics of this large group of students who impact the ethos of a school community.

Characteristics of Bystanders

Who are these bystanders, and is there such a thing as an "innocent bystander"? Gianetti and Sagares (2001) take the position that anyone who stands by and allows others to be harmed is not innocent. So what are they then? Jeffrey, Miller, and Linn (2001) call students who witness the bullying of others secondary victims, proposing that the climate of fear and intimidation created by bullying affects everyone, not just the direct targets of the bullying. It is folly to think that children who observe bullying or are only minimally involved in bullying activities are not affected by their experiences. Their exposure to bullying can lead to a range of feelings including fear, sadness, anger, guilt, and shame.

Some bystanders are not so passive but actively encourage the bullying by their presence, laughter, comments, and general support of the bully. A few of these students are bully "wannabes," who admire the power and presence of the bully, desire his or her friendship, and seem to enjoy the spectacle. Even if bystanders initially start out neutral, it is difficult to continue to be in the midst of bullying incidents and still remain neutral. Eventually, some children become more active participants such as in the example at the beginning of this chapter. This is especially true if a particular student becomes the scapegoat of the class and, therefore, becomes diminished in the eyes of all the students.

Some bystanders are not so passive but actively encourage the bullying by their presence, laughter, comments, and general support of the bully.

Atlas and Pepler (1998) found that peers are present in 85% of bullying episodes, but only intervene to stop bullying 10% of the time. Nevertheless, 90% of children who observe bullying report that they find it unpleasant and disturbing to watch (Ziegler & Pepler, 1993). This obvious difference between students' feelings about bullying and their subsequent actions (or lack of action) should cause us to look for the underlying reasons for why children don't take action when they witness bullying incidents. Garrity et al. (2000) calls bystanders the "silent majority" and points out that the key to bullying prevention is in shifting this group into a "caring majority" (p. 269).

In order to do this, we need to understand why more bystanders don't act either by walking away, supporting the target, and/or directly confronting the bully. There is no one reason, but certainly fear of retaliation, uncertainty as to what action should be taken, and lack of predictability about whether they will receive adult support are important factors in bystanders' decision-making process.

Bystander Roles

As stated earlier, some bystanders are more involved in bullying actions than others. Let's take a closer look at bystander roles. Bystanders can reinforce the bullying behaviors by providing an audience for the bully *(reinforcers)*. For example, when Isabelle is teased and called names in the hall between classes, the bystanders who gather around and watch without saying anything are reinforcers.

Bystanders can become more actively involved and actually provide either physical or psychological assistance and support to the bully or bullies *(assistants* or *supporters)*. Thus, bullies typically have a few friends who consistently support their activities. For instance, Emma usually plans the next attack against Isabelle and tells her friends Mei Li and Anna how they can help. Mei Li and Anna are always in charge of looking out for teachers or other adults. Typically, Emma, Mei Li, and Anna wait by Isabelle's locker. Emma starts the name-calling when Isabelle arrives at her locker to get supplies for her next class. Mei Li and Anna usually laugh and "accidentally" bump into Isabelle as she tries to get to her next class. Emma often trips Isabelle, and at least once a day Isabelle ends up dropping her books and is late for class.

Bystanders can also become actively involved in defending the target *(defenders)*. Unfortunately, students who defend the target comprise a minority of bystanders.

Trisha has three classes with Isabelle. Even though she and Isabelle are friends, Trisha is afraid to say anything to Emma, Mei Li, and Anna because they are known to be very persistent and mean to anyone who dares cross them. Trisha understands that they will probably start targeting her if she takes up for Isabelle. It is hard to watch Isabelle get bullied every day, and once or twice Trisha has said, "Why don't you guys give her a break today?" Most of the time she tells Isabelle in private that the girls are just being jerks and that they should try to avoid them. Whenever she can, Trisha brings Isabelle's supplies to the classroom so Isabelle can avoid going to her locker.

Finally, bystanders can function passively as outsiders, who either do nothing or stay away *(outsiders)*. Many of the students know what is happening to Isabelle. They see what is going on in the hall but avoid the situation and keep walking. They try to avoid eye contact with everyone involved because they just want to stay clear of what is going on. They are disturbed by what they see and worry about what they would do if something like that happened to them. They feel sorry for Isabelle but thankful that they are not being bullied.

As illustrated, most of the time, bystanders function in the role of outsiders (Gianetti & Sagarese, 2001; Jeffrey et al., 2001; Olweus, 1993; Rigby, 1996). Table 6.1 summarizes these bystander roles.

TABLE 6.1
Bystander Roles

- **Reinforcers** – reinforce bullying behaviors by providing an audience for the bully

- **Assistants or supporters** – become more actively involved and actually provide either physical or psychological assistance and support to the bully

- **Defenders** – become actively involved in defending the target

- **Outsiders** – function passively as outsiders, who either do nothing or stay away

---

The fact that none of these bystanders ever reaches out to adults for help is very telling. Many students are reticent to go to adults. In the next section we will explore this culture of silence related to bullying in our schools and neighborhoods.

Culture of Silence

There is an apparent code of silence in schools regarding bullying. Smith (1991) calls bullying the silent nightmare because of this cloud of secrecy surrounding it. In other words, bullying is disturbing to most children, but they suffer in silence because there is a culture of silence in schools and neighborhoods that discourages them from seeking help. Along with this pressure comes a general lack of predictability about how adults and peers will respond when they do ask for help.

. . . bullying is disturbing to most children, but they suffer in silence because there is a culture of silence in schools and neighborhoods that discourages them from seeking help.

The range of feelings that have been noted in children who witness bullying provides important insights into the lack of intervention or response on the part of bystanders. One study identifying the emotions associated with peer maltreatment (victim, aggressor, and observers) found that although empathy was specific to bystanders, bystanders also shared some emotions with both the victims and the aggressors. The emotions bystanders shared with victims were helplessness, confusion, upset, and anger. With aggressors, bystanders shared indifference and happiness (del Barrio, Gutierrez, Hoyos, Barrios, van der Meulen, & Smorti, 1999).

Feelings of indifference and happiness may explain why only a small number of bystanders intervene when bullying occurs, but what about the greater majority of bystanders who appear to feel compassion?

As discussed under bystander roles, these students are afraid and/or not sure what to do when they witness bullying. In reality, there is no way to guarantee the physical and/or psychological safety of bystanders who report bullying. Therefore, many of them remain immobilized by their fear and anxiety, which are greatly enhanced by their lack of certainty about what kind of support and response they will receive from adults and other peers if they report bullying.

Many students predict that adults either cannot or won't help. Parents often reinforce these concerns by telling their kids it is okay and even wise to "stay out of it." All of these uncertainties reinforce the culture of silence.

Factors That Affect Bystander Reactions

Even though the majority of students are (a) opposed to bullying, (b) perceive bullying as undesirable or disturbing, and (c) believe bullying should be stopped, most students do not act to prevent or interrupt bullying. Anecdotal evidence from parents, students, teachers, and other school staff identifies many factors that can affect bystander reactions. Table 6.2 summarizes some of these factors. Many of the factors are related to the issues and concerns discussed in this chapter.

TABLE 6.2
Factors That Affect
Bystander Reactions

Bystanders may:

- Be afraid of retaliation
- Feel a sense of relief that they are not being targeted
- Be unsure of what they are witnessing
- Be unaware of how they are inadvertently supporting bullying
- Feel a diffused sense of responsibility in a group
- Desire protection from the bully
- Hurry past bullying because they do not know what to do
- Be concerned for their own reputation
- Fear for their own safety
- Have been told by their parents not to get involved
- Be amused or excited by the drama of the bully-target interaction
- Feel like someone else can do a better job of helping
- Feel guilty and ashamed for not helping the target
- Stay focused on classroom activities and ignore bullying
- Become afraid of certain places in school
- Feel peer pressure to go along with the bully or to keep quiet
- Perform negative actions in a group that they would not do on their own
- Dislike the target or feel she provoked the bullying
- Feel the target should do more to take up for him/herself
- Talk to their friends about bullying but not adults

Bystanders are an important dynamic in the phenomenon of bullying in our schools and communities. Bullying is not just an experience between two people – bully and target. It is a complex process of behavioral interactions that may involve many children. Since bystanders make up the majority of students at any given time, they have a numerical advantage and, therefore, have great potential for making an impact on bullying prevention. Thus, if we can effectively address their concerns and needs, we can help them become a positive force in bullying prevention.

Consequences for Bystanders

There are at least two major reasons why understanding bystander psychology is critical to bullying prevention and preventing potential long-term consequences for those in the role of bystander. First, when children passively observe the victimization of others, they are learning to passively accept injustice. This goes against the values that our society is based on. Justice and the fundamental, innate rights of individuals are integral components of our society. Second, the behaviors of bystanders can either support/maintain bullying or be a positive force behind bullying prevention. Tapping into this force can make a great difference in changing the attitudes and behaviors in a school and in the larger community (Jeffrey et al., 2001). Without adult support, however, students will be poorly prepared to respond to bullies and remain fearful and uncertain (Batsche & Knoff, 1994).

"For bullies, victims and bystanders, bullying is a formative social experience with long-term developmental implications" (Jeffrey et al., 2001, p. 145). In other words, bullying affects almost every child in school and the lessons learned impact their social development in various ways. If their experiences are negative, the consequences can be serious and affect them into adulthood. Even if a child is only a witness to a serious bullying incident, it can have both short- and long-term consequences.

Implications for Children
with Asperger Syndrome

Since children with AS typically have a lower social standing and often lack a strong social support group in school, they tend to be alone more. As a result, they are less likely to benefit from any protection friends may provide against being targeted for bullying. Further, even though a bully may target a child who is with a friend or in front of other students, it is much easier and less risky to target a peer who is alone and does not have strong peer support.

If other peers are present when bullying occurs, the bystanders are more likely to feel socially connected to the student doing the bullying than with the child diagnosed with AS. Bystanders often perceive that they have more to lose if they help the child with AS and little to gain. They may also believe that the child with AS provokes others and deserves to be bullied or teased in return.

Boys who are bystanders may feel disdain, embarrassment, or even anger toward the target if he is a boy because they think he is reacting too passively and acting like a "wimp." Girls, on the other hand, may feel they cannot risk being associated with the target if she is a girl because it would hurt their social status or they would "fall out of favor" with their social group.

A whole-school approach to bullying prevention that promotes a more caring, tolerant community will help students and adults increase their awareness of bullying as well as their knowledge and willingness to take a proactive approach to curb bullying activities. A key factor to bullying prevention success is the extent to which adults and peers recognize bullying when it occurs and take measures to address it in a proactive, predictable way.

Chapter 7 discusses how to gather information from school staff, students, and parents as part of the effort to create a bullying prevention program and special considerations for students with AS, including busting bullying myths.

PART TWO

Taking a Stand Against Bullying

CHAPTER 7

Increasing Awareness and Understanding

Gathering Information on Bullying

The information discussed in the first six chapters provides a foundation for increasing a general awareness and understanding of bullying. In addition, each school community must individualize and determine how to best use their resources (money, staff, expertise, time) based on their own distinctive issues and concerns, such as whether to hire an expert on bullying and bullying prevention to assist with staff training.

This chapter includes a discussion of considerations for gathering information about bullying from school staff, students, and parents, as well as how to individualize assessment for children with AS to determine their social experiences. This process will help identify what bullying myths are alive and well in the school community and, at the same time, create a strong foundation on which to build a successful bullying prevention program.

Gathering Information From School Staff

As emphasized throughout this book, awareness and commitment from adults is a prerequisite for the success of any bullying prevention program. As a first step, it is critical for the school administration to support efforts to obtain information about bullying from staff. The attitudes and beliefs of school administrators will have a tremendous impact on whether teachers and other school staff feel supported and motivated to embrace an effective bullying prevention program.

It is imperative to obtain information from school staff, including administrators, teachers, counselors, office staff, resource officers, school nurses, food services employees, bus drivers, and anyone else who may be required to intervene when bullying incidents occur. This assessment process ought to include information about attitudes and beliefs concerning when, where, and how often it is believed that bullying occurs in the school, along with what role respondents believe adults should take in preventing and intervening in bullying incidents.

What the Research Tells Us

According to recent research, teachers and other school staff are typically unaware of the extent of bullying in their school. Thus, teachers report they "almost always" intervene in bullying incidents 71% of the time compared to student reports of 25%. However, observations have indicated that teachers actually intervene in only 14% of classroom episodes of bullying and only 4% of playground episodes of bullying. Possible reasons for this low teacher intervention rate may be that bullying is a covert activity. That is, many episodes are brief and verbal, and commonly occur when there is a lack of supervision (Pepler & Craig, 2000).

Clearly, what teachers and other school staff believe constitutes bullying behavior and what roles they believe they should take in response to bullying incidents are vital factors related to what appears to be a vast underestimation of bullying in schools. If teachers and other school staff are present when bullying occurs and fail to intervene, students become more fearful and unable to predict their environment and the actions of others. In fact, students may predict that adults will not intervene and, therefore, develop a sense of hopelessness and apathy. This is obviously counterproductive to the goals of bullying prevention.

Information can be gathered with an anonymous survey or through small-group discussions. More than one approach can be utilized such as surveying teachers, bus drivers and other identified support staff, as well as establishing small-group discussions for classroom teachers. Small-group discussions can help identify individual teachers who may be interested in taking a more active role later, perhaps as a member of a coordinating group.

Information can be gathered with an anonymous survey or through small-group discussions.

Garrity et al. (2000) provide a comprehensive approach to bullying in their book, *Bully-Proofing Your School: A Comprehensive Approach for Elementary Schools.* The book contains many reproducible forms, including the Colorado School Climate Survey for elementary school staff (also available for secondary students). This is a set of questions that asks school staff to tell about their school and "things that may or may not have happened" pertaining to bullying (pp. 69-71). A Bus Driver Survey and a Bus Rider Survey are also available. Check the Resource section for more information.

Information gathered from school staff can be shared through a written report, during staff meetings, and/or during a designated staff-training day (see Chapter 8 for a more detailed discussion of interventions at the school level).

In many cases, teachers feel that most of their peers hold views similar to their own and that they intervene in comparable ways when bullying occurs (Garbarino & deLara, 2002). However, they may be shocked to find that their fellow teachers have very different views about what constitutes bullying behavior and what types of bullying occur in their school, as well as where and how often it occurs. The most surprising insight, however, may be the information about how other teachers deal with bullying when it occurs.

Recent research (Garbarino & deLara, 2002) reports the results of interviews with teachers about what they consider to be bullying behavior, their role in bullying intervention, and the methods they use to intervene. Teacher responses varied greatly, and although all teachers agreed that school should be a safe place for students and teachers, they differed significantly on what constitutes bullying, how to accomplish the goal of providing a safe environment, and what roles teachers should be responsible for in the process.

This is exactly why gathering information is a vital first step in bullying prevention. It will help clarify the different perceptions held by adults and students about bullying. Also, it will give a very clear picture of what needs to be included in the training process and perhaps some areas where reeducation is needed. For example, if the information gathering indicates that teachers feel that students should be able to work things out themselves and that they do not consider it part of their responsibility to monitor student behavior in hallways, this has important implications when subsequently developing policies and intervention plans.

Gathering Information From Students

Gathering information from students is perhaps the most important part of increasing awareness and understanding. Indeed, it would not be unexpected for teacher and student reports to vary significantly during the information gathering stage (Garbarino & deLara, 2002; National Association of Attorneys General, 2000; Pepler & Craig, 2000).

Surveying Students

Students are key when gathering information about bullying activities. They know who is being bullied, who the bullies are, and where the unsafe places are in the school. They can also provide insights into how they feel about bullying, including the all-important silent majority of students who typically stand by and observe from the safety of the sidelines.

Most researchers agree that an anonymous questionnaire is the most efficient and effective method of surveying students. However, consideration must be given to the specific characteristics of the students surveyed. Some students, including children with AS, are very literal and have difficulty with nonverbal communication and social language. Therefore, questionnaires need to take these characteristics into consideration, including possibly modifying content and/or administration.

Schools need not design their own surveys. Student questionnaires are available that help assess bullying in schools. For example, all the bullying programs listed in the Resource section of this book include ways of obtaining information from students. Specifically, the book *Bully-Proofing Your School* provides a handout for the Colorado School Climate Survey for students. This set of questions asks the student to provide information about their school and "things that have happened to them or other students" (pp. 55-61). Suggested time for completion is only 30 minutes; it is strongly recommended that the questions be read to students to help ensure understanding regardless of the reading level of students.

A new survey can be developed or an existing questionnaire can be modified to accommodate the special needs of children with exceptionalities such as students with learning disabilities or pervasive developmental disorders.

Modified Inventory of Wrongful Activities

I chose Brown's (n. d.) Inventory of Wrongful Activities (I.O.W.A.) as an example of a comprehensive student survey available on the Internet, http://www.safeculture.com/iowa.html, that could easily be adapted to accommodate for some of the differences in children diagnosed with AS. The new adapted version, Modified Inventory of Wrongful Activities, is available in the Appendix. Similar modifications could be used with other available questionnaires.

In this modified version, questions and responses are stated concisely, and examples are typically given when social language or nonverbal communication is involved. There is no attempt to shy away from collecting sensitive information, and frank examples, descriptions, and/ or definitions of terms and types of bullying are dealt with in a direct, informative manner.

A sample item of the Modified Inventory of Wrongful Activities illustrates the level of specificity recommended. "Used hand signals to be mean (like making an 'L' with their fingers and putting it on their forehead)" or "Insulted me with sexual talk or jokes (could include hand signals like raising the middle finger or name-calling like 'slut' or 'fag')." This questionnaire is probably best suited for older elementary, middle, and high schoolers. Even though some of the language may seem harsh, it is a mistake to shy away from gathering this type of sensitive information because it reflects an unfortunate reality for students in our schools.

Individualizing Assessment for Children with Asperger Syndrome

These simple modifications make the questionnaire more user friendly to children with AS and many other students with special needs as well. However, even with modifications such as these, most students with AS will require more individual assessment to adequately evaluate their social experiences. Since children with AS are at considerable risk for chronic, frequent, and severe bullying, they should receive individual instructions before completing a survey and be individually interviewed about bullying as well. That is, after children with AS complete the survey, individual interviews using the survey as a guide will help ensure a more complete picture of their social lives.

I have discovered some limitations and concerns in administering the Modified Inventory of Wrongful Activities to students with AS. Some students with extensive histories of being targeted for bullying per parent and teacher reports did not check any of the items indicating that bullying had occurred. One teenage student with AS who responded in this manner wrote in the comment section at the end of the survey:

> *"The reason I had not checked the first section of the questions about people being mean to me in the school is because no one has been mean to me there. That is why I never checked any answers to that section. I've had severe bullying problems in the past, just not this year. I've learned techniques to control my anger (not to fight back), and my parents have been working with school staff to help."*

What a wealth of information this 16-year-old student provided with his comments. None of this information would have been discovered through the questions on the survey because they only asked what bullying experiences he had encountered this year. Further, another student with AS, especially not a younger student, may not have offered this information in the comment section.

A 16-year-old female student with AS also responded to the survey by not marking any of the questions concerning bullying experiences. She also chose to write in the comment section and wrote the following:

> *"I have never, at my high school, had the opportunity to see how a teacher might act in response to students being mean because, while I'm sure that that has happened, it wasn't in front of me. I know that that is totally unlike most people's experience at school, but that's how it is at mine."*

These comments are important because they point to the need for further investigation. For example, it would be important to follow up to determine if this student understood that the questionnaire was asking whether she had ever been bullied, and equally important, to find out if she is able to recognize bullying when it occurs.

Both of these examples verify that individual interviews are necessary when gathering information from students diagnosed with AS. This is not surprising in light of the fact that these students have a social-communication disability.

Other methods of assessment such as social autopsies can also be used. A social autopsy is a method of gathering information by dissecting a specific social situation after it has occurred. This helps increase understanding and provides another avenue for identifying bullying situations and eventually developing individualized strategies for the student with AS (Bieber, 1994; Simpson & Myles, 1998).

Gathering Information From Parents

Parents can also provide essential information about the experiences of their children and should be included in all phases of developing a bullying prevention program. As discussed in Chapter 1, bullying is not just an experience between two people (bully and target) but a complex interaction that must be viewed within an environmental perspective. Clearly, family is an important factor in this dynamic.

Parents can be drawn in from the beginning by providing them a means of relaying information about their own beliefs and attitudes and the experiences of their children. This can be done through an anonymous survey or during meetings set up for this specific purpose, or both.

Parents can be drawn in from the beginning by providing them a means of relaying information about their own beliefs and attitudes and the experiences of their children.

An example of a bullying survey for parents of elementary students can be found in the book *Bully-Proofing Your School.* A reproducible handout for the Colorado School Climate Survey for parents consists of questions that ask about the child's school and "things that may or may not have happened to him or her at school" (Garrity et al., pp. 63-67). Resource information for students in secondary school is provided in the Resource section of this book.

Many parents appreciate the opportunity to voice their concerns and ideas in a constructive manner. After this initial information gathering stage, it is important also to give parents the opportunity to become involved in policy planning and implementation. Parents have much to offer and will be more likely to "buy into" a program when they feel actively involved in the process.

A Strong Foundation

Gathering as much information as possible from school staff, students, and parents will build a strong foundation on which an effective bullying prevention program can be established. Among other things, the information gathered during this stage will help identify what bullying myths are alive in a particular school. Commonly held myths include such wrong thinking as "boys will be boy," "what doesn't kill you makes you stronger," "just ignore it and they will stop," "he/she probably had it coming," "just give back as good as you get," "some children just let themselves get bullied," and so on. Check out the website, Staci's Place-Anti-Bullying Page at http://www.brandjasmine.com/web/staci/myths.html, for a listing of bullying myths and information that provides a reality check for busting these myths.

The goal of gathering information and increasing awareness is to make sure that all types of bullying are recognized by adults and students as unacceptable. In the remaining chapters I will discuss how information presented in Chapters 1 through 7, along with information gathered from a particular school, can help build a successful bullying prevention program. Strategies that can be used at the school, class, and individual level will also be examined along with special considerations for children with AS and their families.

CHAPTER 8

Bullying Prevention at the School Level

Establishing a Bullying Prevention Program

Involving school staff, students, and parents in developing a whole-school approach to bullying prevention is absolutely essential, although not always easy. In this chapter, I will discuss strategies for implementing a successful bullying prevention program at the school level, including staff training, developing goals and a school code of conduct for bullying, creating a coordinating group specifically for continued involvement in bullying prevention issues, strategies for enforcing the code of conduct, and how to involve students and parents throughout this process.

Training for School Staff

Bullying prevention is an ongoing process, not a one-time campaign. When the school district and administrators decide to launch a schoolwide bullying prevention program, staff should be brought together by school administrators for the purpose of presenting the results of information gathered from staff, students, and parents as well as for increasing awareness and understanding about bullying and bullying prevention.

Inservice on Bullying

It is optimal to devote at least a half day, or preferably a full day, for training and education about bullying. It is recommended that a speaker who is familiar with the topic and can speak knowledgeably about bullying in schools be invited. Sometimes outside speakers are more readily accepted as experts because they are not already embedded in another role in the school community. If an outside speaker is not brought in, a person or persons within in the school will need to take on this responsibility. While counselors are often assigned this responsibility, it could be handled by any other staff member who is knowledgeable about bullying and is comfortable explaining the results of the analysis of the staff, student, and parent surveys.

Regardless of who ends up conducting the training, it is recommended that key points about bullying be presented, supported with results from information gathered from staff, parent, and student surveys and any other means, such as observation of students in a variety of school settings. Information can be supported with statistical information or quotes from students and/or parents written in the comment section of the survey. Direct quotes related to real bullying experiences are often quite compelling. In addition, written information is extremely helpful as a resource that can be referred to throughout the school year. This could be accomplished with handouts and/or a companion book with a focus on a whole-school approach to bullying prevention.

During these discussions, special attention should be given to disparities between staff and student perceptions and what kind of training or responses may be indicated. For example, students may report that one of their main concerns is bullying in the classroom and that they feel teachers are unresponsive to bullying when it occurs, compared to teacher reports of very little bullying during class time and responses indicating that teachers feel they are very proactive when bullying occurs. Such differences in perspective point to an underestimation of bullying by the teachers, which follows closely what the research on bullying tells us.

During staff training it is also the time to identify the most critical areas of need and to prioritize concerns. For instance, if student feedback indicates that students do not feel safe in the hallways between classes and in the locker rooms, it is essential to discuss how to increase proactive adult supervision in these high-risk areas.

An important part of this training is allowing sufficient time for staff to hear feedback about what is going on in their own school and to have time to discuss and brainstorm solutions. It is usually better if the school staff is actively involved in creating viable solutions as opposed to the speaker presenting a specific plan as the best way to proceed. Solutions that have staff support have a greater likelihood of being successful. Table 8.1 lists topics that should be covered during staff training on bullying.

TABLE 8.1
Topics for Staff Inservice
and Training on Bullying

- Definition of bullying, types of bullying, and where and when bullying typically occurs
- Characteristics of bullies and targets
- The role of bystanders and their importance in bullying prevention
- Consequences of bullying for targets, bullies, and bystanders
- A summary of results obtained during the information gathering stage from staff, students, and parents
- Strategies for addressing bullying behavior, including formative and prosocial consequences
- Examples of ways to integrate antibullying material into the curriculum and during class meetings
- A plan for disseminating information about bullying prevention to students and parents
- Establishment of a coordinating group that will follow up on bullying prevention and share information with staff, students, and parents (comprised of staff, students, and parents)
- Creation of a school code and bullying prevention goals
- Special considerations for children with exceptionalities

An agenda can be created using these topics and individualized for a particular school dependent on how much time is provided for the bullying inservice. Schedules may need to be divided into more than one training session, and some topics may be emphasized more for a particular school based on its particular needs. For instance, if the school has previously focused on mostly punitive measures in response to bullying, more time may be required to address how to provide support for prosocial and/or formative consequences. These discussions will naturally lead to the creation of goals for bullying prevention.

Developing Goals for Bullying Prevention

Before specific strategies or interventions are established and implemented, it is important to determine goals for bullying prevention. The following four main concepts will drive the formation of goals for a whole-school approach to bullying prevention:

1. Bullying behavior in all forms is unacceptable, and the fear it causes impacts student learning in a detrimental way.
2. Bullying is occurring in school and it can have serious consequences for many students, especially vulnerable are those who experience chronic, frequent, and severe bullying.
3. Adults, especially teachers, are the most important determinants of successful implementation of bullying prevention and intervention.
4. There is reason to be optimistic that applying new practices and policies will curb bullying activities.

Table 8.2 presents examples of goals that can be incorporated into a whole-school bullying prevention program based on these fundamental principles. Goals will be discussed during this initial staff training and then further developed during follow-up meetings and/or through a coordinating group discussed below.

Establishing a Coordinating Group

This coordinating group will help keep bullying prevention issues in the forefront as an ongoing priority in the school. It would be ideal if every teacher were involved in frequent, regularly scheduled meetings pertaining to bullying. However, this is often not an option due to staffing and time limitations. Instead, typically, a coordinating group consisting of representative staff members, students, and parents takes on the role of becoming actively involved in bullying issues and playing a proactive role in creating a more positive school climate.

Interested staff members can be identified before, during, and even after staff training, but an attempt to establish a coordinating group during staff training with a small group of committed members is an important first step. This group will take on the critical role of providing other staff with valuable insights, strategies, and updates regarding bullying prevention and intervention. Group members will also provide a means of ongoing communication between school staff, students, and parents.

TABLE 8.2

Sample Goals for a Whole-School Bullying Prevention Program

- To create a strong bullying policy that will be enforced first and foremost by adults

- To empower bystanders who witness bullying activities and do not intervene

- To promote acceptance and tolerance and change the school climate to include all students in meaningful ways

- To recognize the dynamics and complexities involved in bully-target relationships

- To develop intervention programs that will reduce the prevalence of bullying behaviors and create a safer school that fosters positive learning experiences for all students

- To be creative in developing strategies to promote social competence for children who bully, targets of bullying, and bystanders

- To develop ways to help students who bully find more socially acceptable ways of experiencing positive rewards

- To build an effective support system for protecting targets of bullying

Developing a School Code of Conduct

As suggested in Table 8.1, establishing a school code of conduct will also be addressed during staff training. An effective code of conduct need only include about three to four important rules as both students and adults are more likely to embrace something brief and to the point. This is in no way meant to imply that bullying prevention is simplistic. Continued education and creative strategies will play an important role in any successful program.

Table 8.3 contains a sample code of conduct that can serve as a guideline for incorporating the main concepts that need to be addressed. The school code serves to clarify and underscore that bullying will not be tolerated and that adults will be proactive in dealing with bullying if it occurs.

TABLE 8.3
Sample School Code of Conduct

---

1. Students agree not to bully or tease each other and to treat all students and adults with respect.

2. All school staff will immediately confront bullying and teasing if it occurs and agree to treat all students and adults with respect.

3. Students agree to help those being bullied or teased by speaking out or getting adults' help.

4. All students agree to include everyone in their activities when appropriate. No one is to be intentionally left out or shunned.

After a code of conduct has been established, school staff, students, and sometimes parents can determine creative ways to advertise the code. For example, it can be posted in every classroom as well as in all public areas (restrooms, playgrounds, gym, lunchroom, and hallways). It is helpful if the code of conduct can be incorporated into the current discipline and support structure of the school using already established and successful resources. For example, if students who report bullying traditionally go to the school counselors, this can continue to be an identified support role for counselors related to the school code of conduct for bullying prevention.

Identifying Staff Roles

During the initial staff training, it is extremely helpful to set time aside to explore how to help adults identify their strengths and weaknesses in addressing bullying. Some adults are more comfortable consoling students or teaching strategies than they are with actually intervening and confronting students when bullying occurs. Although all adults must recognize that they are responsible for intervening even if they are uncomfortable doing so, adults who are identified as having strengths in this area are typically more proactive. These are the adults who should optimally be supervising in high-risk areas.

Other adults can provide support by developing creative ways to integrate bullying into the curriculum or teaching strategies to students. For instance, a speech and drama teacher may take an active role in providing opportunities for students to role-play bullying scenarios as part of her class work. Administrators can be supportive by promoting situations where adults can take on roles based on their identified strengths. Nevertheless, all adults should receive some training on how to intervene whenever bullying occurs so they can do so appropriately when necessary.

Since adults are the main driving force behind bullying prevention and intervention, it is imperative that school staff be trained to effectively respond to bullying incidents. It is critical that the importance of immediate and consistent intervention is stressed to all adults who may be in the position of witnessing bullying. In Chapter 9, I will discuss in more detail

> *Since adults are the main driving force behind bullying prevention and intervention, it is imperative that school staff be trained to effectively respond to bullying incidents.*

how to distinguish between playful teasing and bullying and how to respond to bullying when it does occur.

Enforcing the School Code of Conduct

Many factors need to be taken into consideration when determining how to enforce a school code of conduct for bullying prevention. Some of these considerations are listed in Table 8.4. Staff training is a time when these procedures and plans can be initially discussed to be refined later by the coordinating group and in followup meetings.

TABLE 8.4

Considerations When Planning
How to Enforce Bullying Policies

- Develop procedures for reporting, recording, and investigating bullying incidents

- Establish the expectation that staff is to respond immediately when bullying occurs

- Develop procedures for followup and feedback

- Consider the frequency, duration, and severity of bullying when determining consequences

- Utilize counseling staff when possible for children who bully, targets of bullying, and bystanders

- Include formative and prosocial consequences for students who bully

- Be creative in promoting positive social ways for bullies to channel their behavior

- Provide support and individualize strategies for targets of bullying

- Decide who will be responsible for determining and enforcing consequences

- Establish a step procedure (see Table 8.5) to handle the majority of bullying incidents (unless unusual circumstances exist or bullying is severe and chronic in nature)

- Consider the exceptionalities of children when they are involved in bullying incidents

---

Using a Step Procedure

When determining the consequences of bullying behavior, a step procedure can be helpful by establishing consistency in responding to bullying. This allows students to more aptly predict their environment and, therefore, feel safer and more secure. The adoption of a step procedure for students who bully is up to school administrators and staff. An example of a step procedure is laid out in Table 8.5.

TABLE 8.5
Example of Step Procedure for Students Who Bully

First Offense	• Record bullying incident in the student's file. • Counsel student concerning incident.
Second Offense	• Record bullying incident in student's file. • Counsel student concerning incident. • Inform student's parents. • Determine formative/prosocial consequences.
Third Offense	• Record bullying incident in the student's file. • Have a serious talk with the student and his or her parents. • Determine formative/prosocial consequences. • Include counseling and reeducation for the student.
Chronic, Serious Bullying	• Record bullying incident in the student's file. • Have a serious talk with the student and his or her parents. • Determine formative/prosocial consequences. • Seriously consider anger management or conflict-resolution training for student. • Set up counseling (include parents if at all possible). • Take away school privileges (e.g., after-school activities). • Move student out of class if necessary.

The consequences for the first bullying offense focus on counseling and recording the bullying incident in the student's file. If a second offense occurs, a report is made, parents are contacted, and formative consequences are determined. An example of a formative consequence is having students place a phone call to their parents to explain their behavior and determine a specific act of making amends to the targeted child. The third offense also includes serious talks with both the student and his parents, including counseling and reeducation for the student related to bullying and the school code of conduct.

Other prosocial and/or formative consequences may be applied as well. For example, the student may be required to work with younger students in a helping capacity and receive positive feedback from those same students for his help. This will give the student who bullies the power and influence he desires, but in a more positive, appropriate way.

Serious or chronic bullying demands a more severe approach, including consequences that are individualized based on the specific characteristics of the situation. It needs to be emphasized that if it becomes necessary to move a student to a different class, the student who bullies is the one who should bear the burden of having to be relocated. The targeted student should only be moved as a last resort. Unfortunately, there are instances when the bullying in a classroom or school becomes so pervasive and damaging that this becomes an option.

Involving Students in Bullying Prevention

Students are initially brought into the process of developing a bullying prevention program when they complete the survey mentioned earlier. It is important to give students feedback concerning the results of the survey and to make it clear that the school recognizes that bullying is a serious issue and that everybody is united in their efforts and commitment to make the school a safer place for all students.

Student Assemblies

A school assembly is a way of reaching many students at once. Students can be divided according to age groups or students of all grade levels in the school can be assembled at once. The size of the school and number and range of grade levels will impact which grouping is best. This is a great opportunity to invite a guest speaker who is not only knowledgeable about bullying but who can speak dynamically and engage the students. Time must be given to inform the students about the results of the survey and explain how the school will be implementing the bullying prevention program. A second, separate assembly can be used for this part of the process if needed.

Interested students can be invited to serve on the coordinating group as representatives of the student population as mentioned earlier. Also, students will be involved at the class level, as discussed in Chapter 10.

Student Reporting

It is difficult for students to report bullying within the culture of silence that is generally promoted in our schools. An accessible reporting system would enable students to become more involved and to do the right thing. One method is to keep a bullying or harassment log in which students can anonymously report bullying incidents and where they are occurring. An anonymous phone line is being used in some schools. Some students and parents may consider the use of an anonymous phone call more appropriate for serious and/or chronic bullying, whereas a harassment log may encourage more spontaneous use. Parents may be more likely to encourage their students to share information if they feel their students are protected.

Involving Parents in Bullying Prevention

Parents can serve as invaluable resources, and their support of bullying prevention is integral to the measure of success that will be achieved. Table 8.6 summarizes ways parents can become involved in planning and implementing a bullying prevention program in their school.

All the options listed will help parents become more informed and afford them opportunities to be involved. Some parents may want to be members of the coordinating group; others may desire to take a different approach, such as chaperoning at after-school activities.

Communicating with Parents

When the bullying prevention program is established, information needs to be disseminated to all parents so that they understand what the expectations are for their children. This should include roles and responsibilities for all students (children who bully, targets of bullying, and bystanders), as well as the roles and responsibilities expected of adults (administrators, teachers, other school staff, parents).

In addition to encouraging parents to be involved in the survey process, a meeting for parents is essential to inform them of the issues in their child's school and the results of the assessment. The Parent Teacher Organization (PTO) is one vehicle for involving parents. For example, a meeting with a guest speaker could be arranged and co-coordinated by the PTO. The more ownership and involvement parents have in the bullying prevention program, the more cooperation can be expected. Even parents who show no interest in becoming involved in any of these programs will

---

TABLE 8.6
Strategies for Involving Parents

- Encourage parents to complete the parent survey when the students are asked to complete the survey shortly after the beginning of the school year.

- Invite parents to a meeting. Share information from the surveys and present an abbreviated version of information given to the teachers during their inservice.

- Encourage the PTO to get involved by helping bring in an expert on bullying to speak to the parents; include an update on bullying prevention at all PTO meetings.

- Provide options for more extensive training on bullying prevention and motivate parents to participate by making it a prerequisite for being able to work as a chaperone during school activities and/or field trips.

- Provide opportunities for parents to give feedback by making sure there is adequate time for discussion and questions during the parent informational meeting on bullying.

- Send information home through the school newsletter, special mailings, emails, the school website, and the use of voice mail if available for your school.

---

receive notification of the school code of conduct and expectations for students and adults. Some parents may be motivated to attend a meeting about bullying if it is a prerequisite for being able to chaperone at school activities and attend field trips. This is a logical connection because parents functioning in these roles are likely to be in a position to observe bullying behaviors and therefore need to know how to respond.

As mentioned, parents need to be represented on the coordinating group to ensure communication on a regular basis back to the PTO. Newsletters and written information sent home can provide updates and help keep bullying prevention in the forefront. Parents need to be encouraged and given direction on how to reach out to the school when they have bullying concerns. As for students, they may also benefit from an anonymous form of reporting such as a designated phone line.

Evaluating the Success of Your Program

Communication at all levels is important to the success of a bullying prevention program. It takes commitment from many people to make the kind of difference in our schools that is so desperately needed. Keeping good records is part of this process.

Keeping Records

It is vital that schools keep records of all bullying incidents so frequency and progress can be evaluated. It is not unusual, and actually expected, for reports of bullying to increase when a bullying prevention program is first put into place. Typically, this does not indicate an increase in bullying incidents but is more likely due to an increase in reporting, which is desirable. When targets and bystanders embrace "standing up" versus "standing by" in cases of bullying, it is a strong indicator that attitudes and behaviors are changing in a positive direction.

Comparing the Results of Bullying Surveys

Administering the staff, student, and parent surveys again will enable comparisons to be made before and after implementation of the bullying prevention program. For instance, the initial surveys can be administered in the fall shortly after the beginning of the school year and then again closer to the end of the school year. It is also helpful to compare the number of bullying reports, suspensions, expulsions, absences, and discipline referrals, since these are all indicators that may reflect what type of impact a bullying prevention program is having. This information will in turn be helpful in planning future strategies and evaluating future priorities.

In Chapter 9, I will expand our discussion of bullying prevention to include strategies at the class level. This includes establishing a class code, conducting class meetings, and approaches to classroom behavior management. Special considerations for children with AS and specific strategies for dealing with targets and bullies will also be explored. Finally, promoting cooperative learning, adult modeling of appropriate behaviors, successful communication between staff and parents, and the importance of teamwork are discussed as well.

CHAPTER 9

Bullying Prevention
at the Class Level

N ow that we have examined how to implement a bullying prevention program at a schoolwide level, let's explore strategies at the class level. This is where real change can take place, and teachers and students will be the main participants in this effort. Still, it is important not to underestimate how vital the support of administrators, other school staff, and parents are in promoting the success of a bullying prevention program.

This chapter includes information about involving students in establishing a class code, identifying roles and expectations, and conducting class meetings. How to manage classroom discipline, including strategies for dealing with targets and bullies, will also be highlighted. The importance of teachers modeling appropriate behaviors, successful communication, and the value of teamwork are addressed, along with how to promote true cooperative learning in the classroom and special considerations for children with AS.

Establishing a Class Code

A class code about bullying created with student input helps establish meaningful expectations for acceptable student and adult behavior. Student input is the key here, as it results in students embracing the class code as something other than just another rule created for them by adults.

Involving Students

Olweus (1993) suggests that class rules be easy to understand and agreed upon by both students and teachers even if a schoolwide code already exists. Creating class rules is a great way to begin a dialogue with students about different kinds of bullying. The following three rules may serve as a starting point; "we shall not bully other students, we shall try to help students who are bullied, and we shall make a point to include students who become easily left out" (Olweus, 1993, p. 82).

I choose to refer to this process as establishing a class code rather than creating rules. The reason for this distinction is that we cannot establish a rule for every situation, and a class code is a representation of values and principles, not just another set of rules and, therefore, more effectively creates the right kind of atmosphere and expectations.

Identifying Bullying Behaviors, Roles, and Expectations for Students

Statements that are value-based such as the "rules" suggested by Olweus can become more concrete to students, and therefore more effective, by discussing different ways in which students bully, tease, or exclude others. Such a discussion will also help students understand that everyone has a responsibility to actively prevent bullying and that they are in essence promoting bullying behavior if they do not accept this responsibility. Take, for example, the following scenario.

Nasim is a 10-year-old diagnosed with AS attending a public elementary school. Because he uses a lot of "big words" and mostly talks about horticulture, the students have been calling him "Professor Plant." At first Nasim thought they were complimenting him, but now he understands they are making fun of him. A group of five boys keeps the teasing going every day and the majority of the other students join in by laughing when they

*tease. Only a few of Nasim's classmates do not actively partici-
pate; they just ignore the behavior of the other kids. The students who ignore the teasing dread when a teacher is not around
because they know the teasing will begin. Some of them would
like to help, but they worry about how the other kids will react
and are afraid they might become the next target.*

*One day Nasim became so upset with the teasing that he start-
ed yelling and stormed out of the classroom. When the teacher
realized he was missing, she became very concerned, but none of
the students would speak up about what happened. Nasim in
the meantime made it to the playground and was going to walk
home but didn't know the way. School officials had to call the
police, who picked him up two blocks from the school. At that
point he was very upset and crying.*

*Nasim's parents were called, and they came and took him home.
Nasim refused to return back to school and was so traumatized
by the event that he had to be taught at home for the remainder
of the school year. Many of his classmates felt genuine regret
about what happened to Nasim but some of the students, especially the five boys who led the bullying, felt like he was just a
"big sissy and a loser."*

In Nasim's situation, there were many students who could have
made a difference in the outcome if they had simply spoken up to the
teacher or even reported the bullying anonymously. A class discussion
about these types of bullying incidents can help students see the real
consequences of what can happen because of their actions or inaction
and how they can make a difference if they "do the right thing."

Establishing Regular Class Meetings

An important component of bullying prevention involves devot-
ing a specific time to discuss bullying issues, preferably weekly. These
class meetings provide opportunities to educate students about bullying behaviors and what they can do to create a more accepting school
community. It is also a time when students can communicate some of
their concerns.

Focus of Class Meetings

Class meetings allow students the opportunity to contribute to establishing a class code and to create a safer classroom environment. When adults consistently set aside time to make these meetings a priority, students will take notice. Class discussions, role-playing, videos, and guest speakers are some ways to explore bullying and bullying prevention with students. Critical aspects of this process include encouraging as much active participation from the students as possible, really listening to their ideas and concerns, and making the process meaningful to them.

A common complaint among students is that they feel their problems and concerns are trivialized or responded to in an oversimplified way. Don't attempt to give students "pat" answers. Adults who take the attitude that bullying is just "kid stuff" will turn off even the younger elementary-age students. Child-ren and adolescents face issues that are sometimes severe in nature, and they need to engage in serious discussions with adults who are willing and able to counsel them. Children can pick out a "canned" presentation immediately and much of the information will be lost on them if they feel it is not relevant to their own situations.

> *A common complaint among students is that they feel their problems and concerns are trivialized or responded to in an oversimplified way.*

Conflict resolution is an important skill for all students to learn and can have a positive impact on peer relations and bullying preven-tion. Discussions that come up during class meetings typically afford opportunities for modeling and teaching appropriate conflict resolution skills. Conflict resolution and other peace-building skills can be embed-ded into the curriculum and modeled by teachers and other adults throughout the school year. (See the Resource section for more informa-tion about available programs related to conflict resolution.)

Approaches to Classroom Behavior Management

On a day-to-day basis, the environment created by teachers drives much of what occurs in the classroom. No matter what policies and philosophies are supported by the school administration, teachers make the daily decisions that impact the lives of our children. How a teacher approaches classroom discipline is an integral factor in determining what kind of class and school climate will be present, which, in turn, will affect how students treat others.

Systems Versus Principles Approach to Classroom Discipline

Fay and Funk (1995) compare a systems versus a principles approach to discipline policies. These two approaches are similar in that they both establish rules and expect teachers and school staff to take action when a discipline rule is broken, but they tend to diverge at this point, as illustrated below.

Using a *systems approach*, discipline is based on very specific punishments for certain violations and emphasis is placed on consistent enforcement of equal punishments for all students without regard to circumstances or individual differences. Zero tolerance is an example of a systems-based approach to discipline.

A *principles approach*, on the other hand, focuses on an accepted set of values that empowers teachers and school staff to consider individual differences when establishing discipline based on these principles. While the values or principles provide consistency, they allow for individual needs and circumstances to be a part of the decision-making process (Fay & Funk, 1995).

In a principles approach to discipline a teacher consistently addresses behaviors but the focus is not on being fair and equal. Instead, the emphasis is on treating everyone with dignity and respect while consistently promoting agreed-upon principles and values in order to obtain consistent outcomes or results. In brief, the reaction or intervention will vary according to what is needed, not what is equal.

> *For example, Brian (an 8-year-old with AS) blurts out in class that "Mira (a girl in his class) got her hair cut and it looks really weird!" Mira gets very upset, turns red in the face, and starts to cry from her embarrassment and hurt feelings. Brian doesn't notice, and because some of his classmates begin to laugh, he says the same thing again, and then again.*
>
> *Brian's teacher is aware of his social difficulties and understands that his intent was most likely not to upset Mira, and that he was influenced by what he considered an encouraging response from the other students. After the teacher talks briefly to Mira*

and lets her leave the room to calm down, she focuses her attention on the entire class and uses this teachable moment as an opportunity to talk about teasing and the different roles students take in this type of situation. During the discussion, she makes sure Brian understands what happened without taking a punitive approach and the entire class brainstorms what kind of amends might help repair Mira's hurt feelings. In brief, without singling Brian out and punishing him for something that is most likely a manifestation of his disorder, the teacher helps all the students learn a lesson – a lesson about teasing and insights about Brian that may help them be more understanding and accepting of him in the future.

Special Considerations for Special Children

Given that a single classroom typically includes students with different personalities, experiences, family lives, learning styles, and exceptionalities, ranging from gifted to severely challenged, a singular approach to discipline (e.g., systems approach) would create an injustice for most students. For example, when a child with AS has to function within a systems approach to discipline, it is almost always a prescription for disaster. Even students who have an individualized education program (IEP), a 504 Plan, and/or a positive behavioral support plan often find themselves caught up in situations where they are punished when what they really need is guidance and support. If children with AS do not receive what they need, more "misbehavior" will inevitably follow. With regard to discipline, students with AS typically function much better with a principles approach to discipline.

Too often, parents of children with AS are told by teachers and administrators that it is not fair to the other children if they provide a different disciplinary option for the student with AS. Another common experience is when parents of a child with AS are told that it is in their child's best interest to receive the same disciplinary consequences as the other students even when the child's behavior is clearly a manifestation of his or her disability. One of the reasons typically given in such situations is that the child will "fit in" better if he is not singled out in front of his peers. Another reason is that the child with AS will somehow benefit from being punished. To make matters worse, such reactions sometimes occur even when the child's behavior is due in part to a lack of provisions otherwise set forth in the child's IEP or 504 Plan.

For example, if Brian (in the previous example) had been disciplined for blurting out about Mira's haircut and given a one-hour detention after school and a visit to the vice principal's office, what good would have come out of his punishment? More important, did Brian deserve to be punished? Was there intent to harm? What about the other students who laughed and encouraged his behavior? Were they not equally or actually more at fault than Brian? If Brian had just been given a standard punishment under a systems approach to discipline, important interventions that might change attitudes and behaviors would never have happened and Brian would have become a victim along with Mira. Further, if Brian's IEP contains provisions for this type of behavior, failing to implement the plan, and instead punishing the student for a behavior that is a manifestation of his disability, would be totally inappropriate. Unfortunately, this type of outcome occurs often in schools that function primarily from a systems-based approach to discipline.

In Chapter 1, I discussed the pitfalls of zero tolerance. Every parent should be concerned about the proliferation of zero tolerance policies and the zeal with which they are applied to our children. Parents of children with AS who are provided for under general or special education need to be aware that, under some circumstances, their children's educational opportunities are at risk even if the behavior in question is a manifestation of the disability. An example would be the child with AS who verbalizes a threat to either a teacher or a student, or who engages in a violent scene or writes a violent story and is disciplined without regard for her disability.

As mentioned, schools that use a systems approach to discipline set a high priority on *reacting* consistently to incidents. As a consequence, their resources are directed towards providing supervision for after-school, in-school, and Saturday school detentions. Even more resources will be needed for followup, which will likely include extra detentions for students who didn't show up for their detention, communications with parents, and paperwork.

Schools that use a principles approach place a stronger focus on outcomes.

Schools that use a principles approach place a stronger focus on *outcomes*. In other words, when teachers interact with students, they have a particular goal or purpose in mind. Fay and Funk (1995) conclude that most of the time when behavior and learning is involved, a principles approach is

. . . most of the time when behavior and learning is involved, a principles approach is desirable.

desirable. Even if the school's policies are more systems driven, teachers can still treat students with dignity and respect, honor the provisions of their IEPs, 504 Plans, and positive behavioral support plans when available, and be creative in managing behaviors in their classroom.

Let's consider the example of Brian's blurting-out behavior again. Even if this school had a systems approach to discipline that mandated a one-hour after-school detention for misbehavior in class, it is still the teacher's responsibility to determine whether "misbehavior" occurred or whether Brian's behavior was a manifestation of his disability. The teacher decided this was an unfortunate incident that presented a teachable moment and was creative and fair in how she handled the situation. In the long run, this teacher will probably have less discipline problems of this kind to deal with in her classroom because she *stopped teaching to spend a few minutes teaching.*

Paying Attention to Positive Behaviors

Many interactions between students and teachers are driven by attention to negative behaviors or "misbehavior." Children with AS are particularly prone to receiving negative attention based on their challenges instead of positive attention or recognition of their strengths. This is partly because most general education teachers are not typically specialists in how to deal with children who have special learning and/or social-behavioral difficulties and needs. It is further complicated by the fact that special education teachers are trained to identify challenges and tend to focus on how to help children compensate and learn. Therefore, the main focus is once again on students' challenges, not their strengths. Finally, teachers who are trained to deal with gifted or more able students are focused on the students' strengths but often lack the training to deal with learning differences or other challenges experienced by children with exceptionalities as well as children with unidentified needs (Robinson, 1999).

Many children with AS are twice exceptional as a result of having significant strengths in some areas; for example, an incredible rote memory, a focused area of interest, and strengths in science or math, perhaps along with an above-average or even gifted intelligence. However, at the same time they may experience severe challenges in other areas, such as sensory sensitivities, and deficits in social skills and executive functioning. Because of the nature of their abilities and disabilities, children with AS benefit from a team approach that includes teachers from all the above-mentioned areas of expertise. Strategy sharing and continued education on the part of professionals along with large doses of compassion and flexibility ultimately provide the best learning environment for children with AS. A teacher who lacks flexibility and is intent on "controlling" behaviors in the classroom by delivering "equal and fair punishments" is not going to be the most appropriate teacher for a child with AS.

In Chapter 10, I will discuss specific ways that teachers can work as a team in providing strategies for students with AS. It is imperative that we better address the strengths of children with AS along with their weaknesses. A team approach, including general education teachers, teachers of children with special needs, and teachers of students who are gifted, diligently collaborating on producing a successful learning environment will benefit many students, especially children with AS.

What does this have to do with bullying prevention? A lot, because part of what sets students (especially students with AS) apart in the classroom environment is their inability to thrive and function successfully in school. All children have a strong need to belong and if they feel like "misfits," they will either withdraw and feel disconnected and hopeless or act out behaviorally either by seeking attention or by venting their frustrations in inappropriate ways.

Bullying prevention does not happen in a vacuum. If a bullying prevention program is established, it can only be successful if children are met at the point of their greatest need. Children who feel unsafe in school and are not able to learn in a meaningful way due to a lack of support or an absence of challenge, or both, will not be able to meet their potential. All children have special needs and all children should be encouraged and supported to reach their potential.

Responding Immediately to Inappropriate Social Behaviors

Teachers and parents need to become more aware of what is going on socially in the classroom and be ready to step in when difficulties are identified or reported. It is imperative that teachers intervene immediately when bullying takes place. Whenever possible, this should be done in private so that students who are involved can "save face" and to avoid creating more animosity or embarrassment.

This is where staff training in bullying prevention will greatly impact the teacher's effectiveness. A heightened awareness of what types of bullying occur in the school environment and the different roles students take in this bully-target interaction will provide teachers with the knowledge necessary to intervene successfully. Teachers who have the opportunity to role-play how they might respond in bullying situations during their training will most likely be better equipped to act when the actual need arises. An increased awareness on the part of students, parents, and administrators will also promote a supportive environment in which teachers will experience a greater sense of empowerment to help create a more positive social milieu.

Strategies for Dealing with Bullying Behaviors

Dealing with bullying behaviors is challenging for most teachers. The strategies presented in Tables 9.1 and 9.2 have been found helpful for dealing with targets of bullying and bullies, respectively. It is critical that adults intervene immediately and offer support and guidance while modeling the behaviors they are trying to promote in their students.

TABLE 9.1
Strategies for Dealing with Targets of Bullying

- Listen, be compassionate and use a calm voice

- Provide as much privacy as possible

- Take reports seriously and reassure students that they were right to come to you and that you will advocate for them

- Decrease self-blame by identifying the bullying behaviors as wrong and unjustified

- Be proactive in manipulating the classroom environment for success (e.g., helpful peers)

- Look for cues that students may need help developing social competence

- Discuss whether other bullying has occurred

- Continue to monitor behaviors and have a followup conversation with the student

- Take into consideration any exceptionalities and how they may impact bullying situations; individualize strategies accordingly

---

TABLE 9.2
Strategies for Dealing with Students Who Bully

- Stay calm but use a firm, straightforward style

- Provide as much privacy as possible

- Give a brief, clear summary of the unacceptable behavior(s) and consequences, if appropriate

- Note the behavior so a pattern can be established if behaviors continue

- Do not get drawn into arguments or lengthy discussions

- Correct the bully's thinking errors (e.g., blaming the target)

- Identify the target's emotions to help promote empathy

- Consider other ways to help build empathy for the target (e.g., role-play incident with the bully taking the target's role)

- Rechannel the bully's need for power into more positive, socially appropriate endeavors

- Model respect and look for opportunities to pay attention to positive behaviors

- Provide formative/prosocial consequences whenever possible (e.g., making amends)

- Take into consideration any exceptionalities and how they may impact bullying situations; individualize strategies and responses accordingly

---

When two or more students are involved in moderate to severe and/or chronic bullying, other strategies are required. The students who are bullying will undoubtedly try to deny or minimize their actions and avoid taking responsibility. When a group of students are involved, it is easier for an individual student to push responsibility off on someone else – even the target. It is important to talk separately to the target and each of the students who are bullying. Depending on the severity of the incident, it may be prudent to bring all the students involved into an area where they can wait under supervision while each student is spoken to independently. This may prevent students from agreeing on the same "story" or version of the episode. The person in charge of supervising the students while they wait will need to understand and take seriously the importance of not allowing the students to talk to each other.

Successful Communication with Other School Staff and Parents

Whenever bullying occurs, communication and cooperation between staff members can be extremely important. It is helpful to consult with other school staff for at least two reasons: (a) to get another perspective on bullying issues that arise and (b) to alert or communicate problems to colleagues who may need to intervene as well. Do not underestimate parents as a resource but also realize that it is sometimes challenging to discuss an emotional issue like bullying with parents whose own child is bullying others. Some parents are very concerned, creative, and helpful, but others become defensive, deny their child's involvement, and may even become angry.

When dealing with parents who are angry and perhaps concerned about protecting their child from consequences, it is important to matter-of-factly refer to the school and class codes of conduct when explaining why the student's behavior is not acceptable. Focus on how to help the student learn more acceptable behaviors and how this will positively impact her life.

Focus on how to help the student learn more acceptable behaviors and how this will positively impact her life.

It may be necessary to remind parents that children who are allowed to develop bullying patterns of behavior are at high risk for negative consequences in the future, including juvenile delinquency, criminal behavior as adults, and domestic abuse.

It is usually advisable to involve parents early on. Parents do not want to learn that their child has had a long-standing bullying problem and they are being informed only because the situation has become serious; in some cases, their distress would be justified. The same is true for parents of a child who has been targeted for bullying. In brief, bullying behavior that has become frequent, serious, and chronic is much more difficult for everyone involved.

Students who bully repeatedly require anger management classes and individual counseling. By comparison, students who are frequently targeted for bullying or have experienced severe bullying require a tremendous amount of support to help them deal with their anxiety and possibly depression. They may also need help with social skills and making friends. Parent and staff support will greatly impact the success of these strategies. Chapter 10 will present a more detailed discussion of strategies for individual students.

Modeling Appropriate Behaviors in Class

The key to successful bullying prevention is *teaching respect and tolerance for others even when they are different from us.* Students must be educated to recognize behaviors that are hurtful and demeaning to others. Adults will be successful in teaching these vital lessons to students only to the extent that they are able and willing to model these same principles in the school community in their relationships with students and their own peers.

How teachers behave and how they treat their peers and students is reflected in their tone of voice, language, and emotions, and the values and principles they model have more impact than any lecture ever could. There is no one way to teach, but teachers must realize that no matter what activity they are participating in – giving directions, answering questions, checking work, giving praise, monitoring behaviors – they must model the behaviors and choices they want their students to embrace. For example, it would be self-defeating for teachers to insist that their students talk to them respectfully if they themselves use sarcasm or other demeaning behaviors in the classroom. Similarly, if teachers ignore bullying behavior or do little when students come to them for help, they should not be surprised when students do not report bullying or help other students when they are being bullied.

From preschool through high school, adults in the school community must send consistent messages about how to treat others. All students are sensitive to the demeanor of their teachers – the way they work with them as individuals, how they encourage and model cooperative behaviors, and their use of conflict resolution. If teachers rely only on their authority and "might makes right," they can expect that this message will not be lost on their students. Students need to learn cooperative behavior and what better way to learn than by watching the adults in their life model these behaviors (Johnson & Johnson, 1991; Rigby, 1996).

Promoting Cooperative Learning

Working cooperatively is an expected skill for most adult workers in our world today. Even so, schools still embrace competition in the classroom, and students who compete and win are valued highly in the school community. Encouraging competition in the classroom is not conducive to creating positive relationships between students and, instead, tends to set students against each other. It does not take children long to figure out that in order for someone to win, someone has to lose. Students who don't know the answer and don't raise their hand are not even able to compete. Some students quickly learn that they are not going to be successful and, therefore, just give up. Typically, some of these students are students with special needs who perhaps require something as simple as longer processing time to participate more fully.

Exploring more cooperative or collaborative methods is an easy means of promoting better relationships between students and of creating a greater sense of community and tolerance between students in the classroom. Unfortunately, some of the methods used for group work are not truly cooperative but promote an elitist or competitive atmosphere. The creation of groups must be the responsibility of the teacher, not a popularity contest where students are allowed to pick and choose, resulting in some students always being left out. Students who are not valued in the group can be excluded from contributing and group dynamics may even provide a perfect opportunity for bullying and teasing to occur. Students who are at high risk for social exclusion or have other challenges may find group work structured in this manner extremely challenging.

Not surprisingly, this increases anxiety and, therefore, is not conducive to learning. It is likely as well that the students who have difficulty finding a group for classroom work are the same kids who are typically excluded in other activities. Choosing groups is anxiety-provoking for all but the most popular students and is often just one more negative social experience for students diagnosed with AS. These kinds of attempts at getting students to cooperate can potentially backfire and create even more isolation and negative experiences for many students, particularly students with AS. At a minimum, teachers should compose groups and not allow the embarrassing picking and choosing that students will resort to if left on their own.

Teachers will need to not only compose groups to reduce anxiety and exclusion, they will also need to ensure that high-risk students are placed in groups where they are more likely to experience positive interactions. Teachers can improve the likelihood for successful interactions if they provide particular jobs for students; for instance, a student with AS can be assigned to get information off the Internet and verbally report back to the group, as opposed to assimilating ideas and information and putting them in writing, a task many students with AS would have difficulty with. These are just generalizations, and teachers need to consider the individual strengths and challenges of a particular student when manipulating groups for greater success.

Even with these strategies in place, typical group work often falls short of true cooperation. Many unstructured "cooperative" groups take on similar dynamics to those of the larger competitive classroom and school environment. That is, the most motivated and able students tend to take the lead, do the most work, and then feel resentment. The students who are less able or motivated may contribute minimally, learn little, and end up feeling like failures (Aronson, 2000).

Reducing competition and nurturing true cooperation helps create a safer, more accepting classroom environment and allows more students to feel like successful, contributing members of the school community. Such a sense of safety and belonging is an important factor in bullying prevention. Students learn as much from the process of learning as they do from the knowledge or content of their assignments. Let's examine one method of cooperative learning that seems to encourage true cooperation and look at the components of this method that makes it work effectively.

> *Reducing competition and nurturing true cooperation helps create a safer, more accepting classroom environment and allows more students to feel like successful, contributing members of the school community.*

Jigsaw Method

In order for true cooperative learning to take place, it needs to be structured. Ideally, cooperative learning should comprise much of the learning that takes place in the classroom. The jigsaw method is one example of cooperative learning that has worked effectively. I have chosen to illustrate this method because it embraces and honors the diversity of skills seen in real classrooms (Aronson, 2000).

The jigsaw method is set up to ensure that all students play a vital role in the group. Using this approach, the class is divided into small groups of five or six students and given a task to accomplish. Each individual within the group is then assigned a particular topic or piece of information to gather. After students have collected the necessary information, they report back to their group. The assignment is structured so that the only access the other students in the group have to the individual assignments is through the report presented to them by the student assigned to that particular part of the project. Therefore, each student is essential – the other students need their contribution to succeed. If students ignore or belittle others, they will not be able to successfully complete their project.

After each individual student has completed his or her research, they meet with students from the other groups who have the same assignment and work together by sharing information. This helps promote success for students who may have more difficulties gathering the information. After students share information, brainstorm, and become experts on their topic, they practice their presentations for each other. This allows all students to benefit from listening and paying attention to their peers. (The composition of the expert groups can be manipulated with the strengths and challenges of different students in mind.)

After the expert groups have completed their work, the original groups meet again and each student now presents his or her information to the group. This is true cooperative work toward a common goal. By working together on a meaningful goal, students begin to develop empathy for each other. When you start to understand someone on a personal level and learn to value him or her as an individual, you are less likely to harass or exclude him or her.

After several weeks the groups are typically rearranged so that the dynamics can impact a greater number of students. This method is all about learning to take the perspective of another person. While this can be difficult for many students, it is a major challenge for children with AS (Aronson, 2000).

When considering cooperative learning for students with social-communication disabilities such as nonverbal learning disability (NLD) or AS, it is critical to remember that even a basically sound concept such as cooperative learning is only as good as how well it is planned and implemented in the classroom. For these students, a poorly implemented strategy is not just ineffective, it may have disastrous results. Students with AS and NLD are extremely vulnerable to social failures and exclusion, so teachers need to be vigilant to make sure that learning strategies benefit these students instead of harming them.

Tanguay (1999) suggests that the following recommendations be considered when planning cooperative learning experiences for the NLD student:

1. Teams need to be chosen with particular care for the student with NLD and include students who are likely to be supportive.

2. Teams on which students with NLD participate should not be rotated but continued throughout the year to increase the likelihood of forming relationships with group members, thereby encouraging the student with NLD to take more risks.

3. After the student with NLD becomes more comfortable with the group, assigned roles can be rotated so the student with NLD will be able to stretch her comfort zone with the support of her peers.

4. Feedback from the group should be limited to only one constructive recommendation, with an emphasis on positive statements and no tolerance for destructive or overly critical statements.

5. Cooperative learning approaches can be introduced in preschool. They are more effective the earlier they are introduced to students with NLD.

Beyond teaching students to work cooperatively, adults also need to model cooperation and collaboration with other teachers and school staff. Their actions will speak volumes to the students and reinforce what they are trying to accomplish with the jigsaw groups in the classroom.

Teamwork — The Key to Success

The key to successful bullying prevention is teamwork and cooperation. Both adults and students play important roles, and only by working together can real change take place. For example, school staff and parents must remember to communicate both their concerns and successes. When teachers and parents share successful strategies with each other, it is a powerful way to maximize resources and encourage each other to continue making bullying prevention a priority. Table 9.3 summarizes strategies that help promote positive change in school communities.

TABLE 9.3
Strategies That Bring About Positive Change

- Listen and start conversations with students about bullying
- Be empathetic and compassionate and encourage these qualities in your students
- Be proactive and ready to intervene when necessary
- Let students know that they don't have to solve everything by themselves
- Encourage students to report bullying and always follow up
- Whenever bullying or any other type of harassment comes up in conversation, give a clear message that you disapprove; your silence will be taken as acceptance and approval
- Don't expect peer mediation to work in cases of bullying because of the nature of bully-target dynamics, especially the innate power imbalance that is typically present
- Help all students develop assertiveness and conflict-resolution skills and focus more intensely on students who are involved in bullying incidents
- Model the behaviors of respect and tolerance that you expect from your students
- Track bullying incidents and how they were addressed; share effective strategies with others
- Deal with bullying consistently and immediately and focus on outcomes, not punishments
- Always consider the needs of students with exceptionalities when they are involved in bullying incidents

In addition to other benefits, ongoing communication increases accountability on the part of adults and students. Adults who communicate clear expectations for behavior and display those same behaviors themselves when they deal with others, students who communicate their concerns and report bullying when it happens, and a classroom that values each member of the class community are all the result of adults and students holding themselves accountable for being respectful and tolerant of others.

In short, the most powerful component of any successful bullying prevention program is the extent to which we are willing to listen, really listen, to what our students tell us about their social lives. We need to provide students the time and opportunity to tell us about their experiences so we can advocate for them when necessary, as well as teach them how to advocate for themselves.

Chapter 10 deals with bullying prevention strategies for individual students and special considerations for students with AS. The discussion will include how to be proactive and provide clear expectations, distinguishing between normal peer conflicts and bullying, how to talk to students when bullying occurs, providing formative consequences, and promoting social competence. Also, attention will be given to addressing bullying in the IEP, when appropriate, for students receiving special education services.

CHAPTER 10

Individualizing Bullying Prevention with Special Considerations for Children with Asperger Syndrome

Most students are capable of some form of bullying behaviors but some students show a greater tendency to consistently exhibit these types of behaviors. Some students only target the very weakest students at the bottom of the social ladder seen as scapegoats by the class or sometimes an entire grade. Occasionally, students who are targeted over and over begin to display bullying behaviors themselves in response to such treatment. Other students who are targeted by bullies are passive and never react aggressively but can become very emotional when bullied. Still others, the majority of students, are seldom or only occasionally targeted by bullies and do not typically bully other students.

As discussed in Part One of this book, bullying is affected by many factors, including the innate characteristics of the students involved, family dynamics, school climate, and how students feel about their experiences with bullying. Students are typically targeted because of their vulnerabilities; some may be anxious and passive while others display a combination of anxiety and aggressiveness that is seen as provocative; neither group is typically accepted by their peers. Students who bully seek to control and influence others through the use of power and aggression. Students other than the bully and the target are usually present when bullying occurs. They may take on a variety of bystander roles and are influenced by many of the same factors that affect bullies and targets.

All of these students – students who bully, targets of bullying, students who are both bully and target, and students who witness bullying – require intervention from adults to effectively deal with their social environment. Traditional punishment is usually not effective at addressing the underlying issues or even stopping bullying behaviors. Indeed, responding only with punishment may simply send the message, "Do not get caught." Punishment does not change the social climate and the attitudes that help students who bully feel they are gaining power, influence, and other positive rewards for their actions. The entire social climate needs to change before a true transformation in attitudes and behaviors can take place.

Students who are bullied require a tremendous amount of support and protection, especially if the bullying is chronic, frequent, and severe in nature. Students who bully will most likely suffer long-term consequences and society as a whole will suffer because of the patterns of behavior they will take with them into adulthood. Even students who witness bullying need help handling their emotions and fears and learn how to respond more appropriately when bullying occurs.

This chapter will look at how to distinguish between normal peer conflicts and bullying, how to be proactive and provide clear expectations, how to talk to students when bullying occurs, and how to provide formative consequences and promote social competence. Attention will also be given to addressing bullying in the IEP when appropriate for students in special education, specifically for students with AS.

Distinguishing Between Normal Peer Conflicts and Bullying

In order to intervene appropriately when bullying occurs, adults must be able to determine the difference between normal conflict and bullying. In normal conflicts, the students involved are usually relatively equal in power, possibly friends, whereas in bullying, there is typically a power imbalance and no real friendship. In fact, students who are targeted for bullying are more likely to be alone and without peer support. Further, bullying generally, but not always, consists of repeated negative actions that are purposeful, not accidental. In normal conflict there is usually not a pattern of negative actions or any real intent to upset or harm the other student.

Also, in bullying situations there is usually an attempt by the student who is bullying to gain power and control or possibly even obtain material items such as money or games. In normal peer conflicts, generally, the students involved show some willingness to take responsibility for their actions and express sincere remorse afterwards. They are usually also interested in solving the problem and repairing the relationship. In bullying, by contrast, the student who is doing the bullying often tries to shift blame, does not express sincere remorse, and is not interested in repairing the relationship or solving the problem. Quite the contrary, he or she often seems to be enjoying the interaction.

It can also be difficult to distinguish aggression from play fighting. In general, however, in play fighting, students are more likely to alternate roles (e.g., both students chasing each other around the playground) while aggression or bullying usually involves unilateral roles (e.g., one student pushing or chasing another). Also, students who are "playing" usually stay together afterwards, but with true aggression or bullying they most often separate immediately after the incident.

Table 10.1 summarizes how to distinguish between normal peer conflict and bullying.

TABLE 10.1
Guidelines for Distinguishing Between
Normal Peer Conflict and Bullying

Normal Peer Conflicts	Bullying
Students are relatively equal in power	A power imbalance is usually present
Students are possibly friends	There is no real friendship
There is usually no pattern of negative actions	The targeted students are more likely to be alone and without peer support
There is no premeditation to upset or harm the other student	There is usually a pattern of repeated negative actions
Students show willingness to take responsibility for their actions	Actions are purposeful, not accidental
Students express sincere remorse afterwards	There is an attempt by the bullying student to gain power and control, even material items
Students are interested in solving the problem and repairing the relationship	The student who bullies tries to shift blame
Students tend to alternate roles; not just one-sided	The bullying student does not express sincere remorse but often seems to be enjoying the interaction
Students usually stay together after the incident, especially with play fighting	The student who bullies is not interested in repairing the relationship or solving the problem
	Altercation is one-sided, involving unilateral roles
	Students most often separate after the incident

Considerations for Students with AS

Students with AS often misinterpret or fail to understand social situations and are at an increased risk for being manipulated, humiliated, or placed in unsafe situations. Many times what may appear to be inappropriate behaviors or even bullying on the part of the student with AS is simply an emotional reaction to being bullied. Take the following, for example:

Alex is a 16-year-old diagnosed with AS. He has a lot of sensory issues and is particularly sensitive to anyone whispering in his ear. He describes the feeling it gives him as "a painful tickle that makes his whole body shake and stays around even after the words are said." His classmates have picked up on his "weakness." Two girls that sit by him in math class hate it when Alex cracks his knuckles, especially when they are taking a test.

The day after a math test, they decide to "get back" at Alex by whispering in his ears at the same time when the teacher isn't looking. They pull off their plan, and the teacher turns around to see Alex standing up screaming at the girls. He is very angry and upset, and his face is red. The girls are sitting with shocked looks on their faces, trying their very best to look innocent. Alex is sent to the office.

Even though it is important to respond immediately to bullying, teachers and other school staff must carefully evaluate any social situation where students with AS are involved so as to avoid further victimization of the student. Determining what antecedents were present before the observed behavior is always recommended, but it is an essential part of the intervention process when a student with AS is involved.

When bullied, students with AS may react in an unexpected manner, be overemotional, or show little or no emotion. Some students with AS do not even recognize that they are being bullied and are susceptible to being talked into doing things that will get them in trouble or that will make them the object of ridicule.

Some students with AS do not even recognize that they are being bullied and are susceptible to being talked into doing things that will get them in trouble or that will make them the object of ridicule.

The reasons for difficulties in this area are complex, and include the fact that individuals with AS are socially naïve and at a disadvantage when trying to interpret the intentions of others. It is a misconception that students with AS are not interested in making friends and are not affected by peer pressure. In some instances, they are likely to tolerate a higher level of abuse from their peers in exchange for attention or possible friendship. As one young man with AS stated, "I'd rather be with kids who aren't nice to me than be alone, ignored, and invisible."

If a student with AS is involved in bullying others, it is important to examine the behaviors and/or attitudes observed and determine whether the student has a complete understanding of why a given behavior is inappropriate. Many times, students with AS either misinterpret the actions, words, or emotions of others or fail to understand why their own behavior was seen as hurtful or rude in a particular situation. Sometimes they are just trying to mimic behaviors they have seen other, more popular students use when dealing with peers. At times, they are upset with how others have treated them and attempt to retaliate in kind. In some instances, they join in when students are bullying someone else because they are so relieved that they are not the subject of teasing and bullying for a change. Although less common, students with AS may even initiate bullying someone else to keep from being bullied. That is, they bully so they won't be the one getting bullied. The following is an example of a student with AS trying to mimic the behaviors of his peers, which gets him in trouble with his teacher.

Lavar is an 11-year-old diagnosed with AS. He is in the fifth grade. One day recently while he was swinging at recess, two of his classmates came up to him smiling and said, "Can I see Uranus?" Lavar didn't understand what they meant and repeated back the same question, "Can I see Uranus?" The two boys were amused and started laughing at him and called him "gay boy."

Lavar didn't know why they were laughing but thought maybe it was a joke, so he set off to say the same thing to someone else. He went to find the popular boys playing basketball and kept saying, "Can I see Uranus?" At first they laughed and called him gay, but then they became annoyed and sent someone to tell on him. Lavar ended up having to go in and write up an incident report on what happened. He still thought he was talking about a planet but didn't know why it was funny or why the boys called him gay when he said it. He stated later that he "wanted to say it to someone else so he could figure out what it meant and why it was funny." None of the other boys got in trouble even though Lavar wrote down every detail of the incident, including how it began.

Avoid Blaming the Target

Lavar's experience is typical of many students with AS who get into social situations that they don't totally understand and are easily "set up" and manipulated by other students. Interventions for students with AS need to focus on assisting them in developing skills that will aid them during challenging social situations and help provide for their safety. We cannot overstate how critical it is that adults in charge do not inadvertently escalate matters when students with AS are already anxious and upset by reacting in an overly aggressive or angry manner (Myles & Southwick, 1999). If this occurs, the students with AS will be twice victimized because the very adults who are supposed to understand their challenges and help guide them are placing obstacles in their way. Take a look at the following example:

Lashanda is a 7-year-old diagnosed with AS. She is usually alone at recess, and instead of playing with the other students, she spends her time walking on the border surrounding the play area. She thinks about her favorite videogame and replays it over and over in her mind. Lashanda doesn't like the noisy playground and this activity helps her "go away" and relax enough to tolerate recess. The other kids make fun of Lashanda behind her back and enjoy taunting her by coming up every few minutes and asking her if she wants to swing with them. They know she hates to swing and they just enjoy seeing her reaction because Lashanda says the same thing every time, "Go away, I hate to swing!"

Today has been a particularly difficult day for Lashanda because her class has been taking standardized tests all day. At recess, a group of girls decide to try something new with Lashanda. They all go up to her at once and talk at the same time asking her to swing with them. They keep following her around saying the same thing over and over, "Lashanda, come swing with us."

Lashanda starts yelling at the girls and tries to push them away. One of the girls trips on a rock and falls down scraping her knee badly. She begins to cry, which brings over the playground supervisor. Lashanda is still upset and yelling when the teacher arrives. When the teacher asks what happened, the girls tell on Lashanda for pushing and yelling at them. The teacher is very upset and concerned and yells at Lashanda to come with her immediately. Lashanda is so upset she can't comply and runs from the teacher when she grabs for her arm. Other adults come to help and Lashanda is carried into the school kicking and screaming all the way. The principal calls Lashanda's mother, who has to leave work to pick her up. Lashanda is suspended for three days.

Many parents of students with AS relate that when they bring instances of bullying and harassment to the attention of teachers and administrators, they are advised to tell their child to ignore the bullying behavior. These parents are distressed that there is typically an overemphasis on how their child reacts to bullying. For example, they are often advised that the bullying will probably stop when their child reacts more appropriately. Many times parents are informed that their child will be punished for his or her reaction to bullying (like Lashanda in the example above), even though no action has been taken to curb the bullying behavior of the other students. Another common experience is for parents to be told that their child provokes other children because of behaviors or individual traits that are clearly a manifestation of their disability.

This tendency to blame the target is all too common when students with AS and their parents complain about bullying and harassment in the school environment. Because students with AS have a social disability, it is usually easy for adults to point their finger at something the student is doing or not doing in a social situation that is causing problems.

As we have discussed, if students feel they are being harassed because there is something innately wrong with them, they internalize this as shame. (The Appendix includes a letter I have written to children and adolescents with AS who are bullied, "Straight Talk About Bullying." The intent here is to help targets of bullying understand that they are not to be blamed and to encourage them to reach out to adults for help and support instead of suffering in silence.)

In Chapter 11, a mother shares how her elementary-age daughter with AS has been humiliated, bullied, and tormented by her peers since preschool, resulting in her daughter sometimes expressing the desire to "die or disappear." At times of deep anguish, her daughter has stated, "I am God's greatest mistake." No child should have to suffer in this way, and adults must make every effort not to contribute to the creation of such profound feelings of self-blame and hopelessness.

How to Talk to Students When Bullying Occurs

When students exhibit bullying behaviors, they need to be told in a matter-of-fact way exactly why their behavior is inappropriate and unacceptable. In doing so, adults must remember to control their own anger and frustration so they can have a more positive long-term impact on student behaviors and attitudes. Especially when adults respond to students who have targeted a student diagnosed with AS, they can easily escalate negative feelings and behaviors if they do not present themselves in a calm, deliberate way. Students with AS do not typically have a strong social support group, and an overly emotional and harsh response by adults towards the bully may actually create more sympathy for the bully and animosity toward the responsive adults and the targeted student.

Avoid an Overly Emotional and Harsh Response

The following is an example of a bullying situation handled in an emotional way that results in the bully and his friends seeking revenge for their "treatment."

Nico is fairly popular with most of the boys in his seventh-grade class. He is on the basketball team and is considered the best player on the team. This week he got in trouble for bullying Daniel, another seventh grader who is diagnosed with AS. Daniel is also on the basketball team but he is probably the worst player on the team. Daniel messed up a play during an important game and Nico verbally attacked him in the locker room afterwards. Nico then took Daniel's uniform and threw it in the toilet, telling Daniel that he didn't deserve to wear it because he played so bad. The coach came in and caught Nico in the act. As he proceeded to lose his temper, he started yelling at Nico in front of his teammates, telling him he was off the team for the rest of the season.

Nico and Daniel both felt humiliated in front of their peers. Their teammates were so upset about losing their best player, they didn't even feel sorry for Daniel. Later, Nico met with his friends on the team and they devised a way to "get revenge." They made a plan to make Daniel so miserable that he would quit the team. They decided that if Nico couldn't play, then Daniel shouldn't play either and that they would show the coach he couldn't "go off" like that at his best player.

Privacy

Privacy is also an important part of any interactions between adults and students involved in bullying incidents. This is true for students in all roles – bully, target, and bystander. If students are unnecessarily embarrassed, shamed, or placed in a compromising situation in front of their peers, they are less likely to change their behaviors and/or advocate for others who are being bullied. However, it is important that adults make it clear to the student who is being targeted that the bullying behavior is being addressed; otherwise, he will not feel protected or valued as a member of the school community. All students are constantly taking note of adult responses to bullying behavior. If there is no response, they may make a variety of assumptions, such as believing that bullying behavior is acceptable and that students will not be taken to task for similar behaviors.

Once it becomes clear that the student(s) involved in bullying understand the expectations for their behavior, adults need to make sure that students also know what to expect if any more bullying incidents take place. For example, the step procedure for enforcing the school code as outlined in Chapter 8 can be explained to both parents and students. Students tend to change their behaviors when they believe they are going to be held accountable. If not, they may have issues that require further intervention such as anger management classes or empathy-building exercises, like role-playing bullying scenarios from the target's perspective.

Providing Formative Consequences

When students continue to bully others even after they understand the expectations for their behavior, including school and class codes, they must experience consequences for their behavior. Similarly, when bullying is serious or chronic in nature, the bully must receive consequences relative to the seriousness of the incident, as noted in the step procedure guidelines. (More serious or chronic bullying demands a serious approach, including consequences that are individualized based on the specific characteristics of the situation.) As previously discussed, an emphasis on punitive measures, including suspensions and expulsions, does not usually serve to change behaviors or attitudes.

Changing the dynamics of the school environment from a culture of silence to an empowered, caring majority is an effective way to decrease the acceptability of bullying and, consequently, diminish the power of the bully. Formative discipline includes consequences that teach or help a child think in a different way and that challenge and change behavior as opposed to mere punitive measures. Prosocial discipline provides consequences that requires a child to do something positive and then receives positive feedback in response (Garrity et al., 2000, p. 434). Both formative or prosocial consequences for students who bully can help promote empathy and provide alternative, more positive ways for them to gain power and success in the school community.

School staff can brainstorm and agree upon appropriate formative or prosocial consequences as a part of the process of establishing a bullying prevention program. Table 10.2 provides examples of possible formative/prosocial consequences for students who bully.

TABLE 10.2
Possible Formative Consequences
for Students Who Bully

- Participation in social skills classes and/or anger management classes

- Removal of privileges (recess, attendance at after-school activities)

- Making amends to the targeted child (replacement of broken or missing items, sincere apology)

- Working in a helper role with younger students (will receive positive feedback from students)

- Promoting identification of the target's emotions by having student role-play the bully-target incident in the role of the targeted child, with an adult

- Performing work for office staff and/or teachers

- Making a call to their own parent(s) to explain their behavior and to determine a "caring act" as a consequence for their behavior

- Meeting with a counselor or other identified adult to process through the bullying incident, identify the target's emotions and the wrong thinking involved, and explore more appropriate choices

---

Adapted from Garrity, C., Jens, K., Porter, W., Sager, N., & Short-Camilli, C. (2000). *Bully-proofing your school: A comprehensive approach for elementary schools.* Longwood, CO: Sopris West, pp. 115-116.

Everybody (including adults) should be held accountable for how they treat others. A critical component of successful bullying prevention is adults taking a closer look at how their own behaviors may be inadvertently creating a less than positive social climate.

Taking a Closer Look at Adult Accountability

When adults take the position that a student, particularly a student with AS, is somehow responsible for provoking harassment from peers, these same adults may unintentionally be modeling these attitudes and beliefs through their behaviors to their students. For instance, in the classroom, students watch how teachers respond to the student with AS when she says something "clueless" or "rude," perseverates in asking questions, monologues about an area of interest, or presents with an annoying habit such as fidgeting or knuckle cracking. If a teacher responds impatiently or with sarcasm, rolls his eyes, makes fun of the student's behavior, or excludes the student from class activities, he is teaching the other students how to treat the student with AS – intentionally or not. Adults need to internalize the belief that no person deserves to be teased, humiliated, or treated disrespectfully and model this to their students and other adults.

There is danger in failing to recognize that some adults contribute to the emotional mistreatment of students by intimidating, ignoring, being overly punitive and critical, using sarcasm or name-calling, belittling students in front of their peers, and failing to intervene when students are bullied, teased, and excluded by their peers. Increased security and discipline such as metal detectors and zero tolerance policies will not help these students fell less alone, rejected, and hopeless. Instead, support, understanding, and respect from the adults they are taught to count on will make a difference.

On the other hand, teachers need to be sufficiently supported by their colleagues, administrators, and parents so they can effectively manage classroom issues. When such support is not available to them, they may become frustrated and, therefore, feel less able to support individual students in their classrooms. Appropriate training on bullying prevention, continuing education related to classroom management and students with special needs, and a supportive administration that prioritizes time for teachers to plan and collaborate with their peers, are examples of the kinds of support that teachers require.

Obviously, teachers and other adults modeling appropriate behaviors and being proactive when bullying occurs are critical to the success of any bullying prevention program. The development of a school code as well as class meetings and a class code of conduct provide the foundation for how students should behave in school.

At home parents can provide expectations for behavior by defining clear boundaries for how others (family, friends, etc.) are to be treated. If parents allow their children to be aggressive and tolerate aggressive behavior with siblings and others in the home and community, this will carry over into relationships in the school environment and therefore weaken the school and class code. Modeling by adults of appropriate attitudes and behaviors in the home will further emphasize expectations. Teachers, other school staff, and parents need to be proactive in addressing inappropriate behaviors whenever and wherever they occur. As mentioned before, if adults do not take action when they witness bullying behavior, their inaction results in implied acceptance of the behavior.

Teachers, other school staff, and parents need to be proactive in addressing inappropriate behaviors whenever and wherever they occur.

Modeling appropriate behaviors is crucial in helping students develop social competence. The next section explores social competence, in particular, how adults can work with students to help them develop social competency skills, which will in turn help curb bullying activities.

Promoting Social Competence

The ideal is a whole-school approach to promoting social competence for all students during their primary and secondary school experiences in coordination with a schoolwide bullying prevention program. When that is not possible, targeted interventions such as anger management classes, role-playing, and direct instruction of social skills for identified students involved in bully-target incidents can positively impact the social climate in a school.

Social competence involves mastering the skills necessary for successful social interactions, including the ability to build and maintain positive relationships with others over time and in a variety of social situations. For students, these important relationships can include parents, siblings, grandparents, and other adult family members, adults (not family members), and of course, peers.

The interpersonal skills necessary to develop social competence include conflict resolution, friendship skills, and prosocial behaviors. Certain individual behaviors or traits are also critical in developing social competence such as social confidence, empathy, the ability to effectively problem-solve, and being able to have self-control and regulate behaviors and emotions (e.g., not being argumentative or reacting with physical violence when angered) (Haire et al., 2002; Schwartz, 1999).

Unfortunately, some schools do not have the support, funding, or staffing to provide a comprehensive program to all students. In such cases, minimally, it is critical that students who are involved in bully-target incidents have access to instruction designed to promote social competence. Whether they are students who bully, targets of bullying, or students who have witnessed bullying, these students will all benefit from social skills instruction.

Students with AS require social skills instruction regardless of whether they have been identified as being involved in bully-target incidents due to the nature of their disability. These students are without question at high risk for being targeted for bullying and require proactive support in developing social competence to provide for their safety in the school environment. This is a need that can and should be reflected in their IEP for those who are in special education. A 504 Plan can address similar concerns for students with disabilities in general education.

Students with AS present unique challenges due to the nature of their disability, and special considerations must be taken when determining what instructional approaches will best serve their needs. Fortunately, social skills programs are available specifically designed to address the needs of children with AS. (A listing of programs that can be used with all students as well as programs specifically designed for students with AS may be found in the Resource section of this book.)

One approach, the Power Card strategy (Gagnon, 2001), can be used to help promote social competence in children diagnosed with AS using their area of special interest. Gagnon (2001) provides the following example of how the Power Card strategy was used with a 12-year-old girl named Suzy diagnosed with AS. Suzy often says exactly what is on her mind when talking with her peers, especially when she is tired or stressed. She gets very defensive when adults (teachers and parents) try to discuss how this creates problems in her relationships and fails to see how the way she talks to her peers and others affects her relationships and contributes to her lack of friends.

Knowing that Suzy is a big fan of Britney Spears, her teacher created a scenario and Power Card using this special interest. As illustrated below, the goal was to decrease the occurrence of rude statements Suzy makes to others.

Britney and Her Fans
by Cassie Jones

Britney Spears loves being a music star, but sometimes it is difficult for her to be nice to everyone. At the end of a long day in the recording studio or after a concert, she is often tired and it is difficult for her to be nice to her fans and friends. But Britney has learned that it is important to smile at people she meets and say nice things to everyone even when she is tired. She has learned that if she can't say something nice, it is better to just smile and say nothing at all. She stops and thinks about comments she makes before she says anything.

1. Think before you say anything. Say it in your head first before saying it out loud.

2. If you can't think of something nice to say, don't say anything.

3. You do not have to say every thought out loud that you think.

Just like Britney, it is important for young people to think before they talk. It makes Britney proud when preteens and teenagers remember to do the following:

1. Think before you say anything. Say it in your head first before saying it out loud.

2. If you can't think of something nice to say, don't say anything.

3. You do not have to say every thought out loud that you think.

From: Gagnon, E. (2001). *Power cards: Using special interests to motivate children and youth with Asperger Syndrome and autism.* Shawnee Mission, KS: Autism Asperger Publishing Co., pp. 37-38. Reprinted with permission.

The importance of empathy has been noted several times throughout this book. Students who bully need to develop empathy for those they target if they are to make credible changes in their behaviors and attitudes. Continuing the discussion of promoting social competence, the next section will focus on how to promote empathy.

Promoting Empathy

Many students who bully demonstrate a lack of remorse for their behavior, try to shift blame, and take the attitude that the target somehow deserves to be bullied and is "asking for it." Such students need to develop empathy. This is done by learning to identify their own feelings, as well as the feelings of others, and by taking into consideration the perspectives of others.

Many programs include a component for promoting empathy. The *Second Step* program is one such prevention program developed to curb aggression and foster social competence in children preschool age through grade nine. This comprehensive, whole-school program uses stories and literature to promote understanding. In addition, it includes such strategies as identifying cues related to a variety of emotions, practice in interpreting emotions, understanding how emotions can change over time, distinguishing between accidental and intentional acts, and discussion of fairness. Every student would benefit from a program that facilitates the development of these important skills (Frey, 2000). More information may be found pertaining to the *Second Step* program in the Resource section and at the Committee for Children website at http://www.cfchildren.org.

At the beginning of our discussion on promoting social competence, I mentioned that all students diagnosed with AS require social skills instruction due to their disability and that these needs should be reflected appropriately in their IEP if they are in special education. Since students with AS are at extremely high risk for bullying, the next section will focus on how bullying can be addressed in the IEP.

Addressing Bullying in the IEP

Addressing bullying in the IEP is an issue that many parents of children diagnosed with AS feel strongly about. Some parents report that even when the school staff agrees that bullying is a concern, they continue to meet with considerable resistance from other members of the IEP team when trying to deal with bullying directly in the IEP.

Little information is available on addressing bullying in an IEP for students with AS, despite the recent explosion of written materials on autism spectrum disorders. Thus, I was only able to find one example of an IEP goal written specifically to address bullying and teasing. While researching an excellent website (www.ldonline.org) for children with exceptionalities, I found the following example but was disappointed at seeing an emphasis on how the student with the exceptionality should react to bullying and teasing.

The example was written exactly as follow:

Joe needs to learn how to deal with peers who tease him.

Provide instructions to use appropriate assertive behaviors when teased by others.

1 hr. weekly, Sept. 5–Nov. 15.

Present Level of Performance:

Once or twice daily Joe reacts inappropriately to peer teasing.

Objectives:

1. *Within two weeks, in role-playing situations, Joe will respond appropriately to staged teasing.*

2. *Within six weeks, Joe will respond successfully in confrontations with peers 50% of the time (self-monitoring).*

3. *Within six months, Joe will respond successfully in confrontations with peers 100% of the time (self-monitoring) and the confrontations will be much less frequent.*

Goal:

Joe will react appropriately to peers.

I am disturbed by this example because I think it represents much of what is wrong with how we often approach students who are faced with bullying and teasing. I am not opposed to teaching skills to students that will help them develop social competence, particularly students diagnosed with AS. However, we cannot continue to place the burden of dealing with bullying and teasing on the least empowered person: the target of bullying. When we approach bullying in this way, we are effectively telling the targeted student that bullying and teasing is a part of life and that there is something innately wrong with the way he is reacting to others – in other words, that he is the problem.

If a student with AS is being bullied and teased, I propose that the current issues with bullying be addressed in the present levels of performance section of the IEP. If the student is experiencing anxiety and stress related to bullying and teasing, this would be included as well. After a clear assessment of the problem, the IEP team can continue by determining how to effectively provide for the student's needs, including selecting strategies that will meet the long-term goal of protecting the student from future bullying and teasing. Such strategies should incorporate any bullying prevention program and policies used by the school and provide individualization for the student with AS. Increasing awareness and providing training for teachers and other school staff to improve their understanding of the challenges experienced by the student with AS can also be incorporated.

The following is one example of how bullying and teasing can be addressed in the IEP of an elementary child diagnosed with AS.

Present Level of Performance:

According to teacher and parent reports, Joe's interview with the school counselor, and his responses on a bullying survey, Joe is bullied and teased more than five times a week. When Joe's classmates were given a social survey, 80% of the students listed Joe as someone they don't like to spend time with and 90% listed him as the person they think most needs a friend. None of his classmates listed him as someone they like to do things with most. Additionally, Joe has expressed to his parents and the school counselor that he doesn't think the teachers like him as much as the other kids and that he doesn't have any friends. Joe seldom reports to his teacher when he is bullied and teased unless the bullying becomes frequent and severe and Joe in turn becomes stressed and anxious. Bullying and teasing occurs most frequently during lunch and at recess.

Goal:

Joe will develop and maintain effective relationships with his peers and teachers and learn to recognize and report bullying and teasing if it occurs.

Annual Goal #1:

Joe will develop and maintain effective relationships with his peers and establish and maintain a friendship with at least one peer in his class.

Short-Term Objective

Joe will identify at least one student as a friend, and when a social survey is given in December, 50% or fewer of his class-

mates will identify him as someone they don't like to spend time with and 60% or fewer will identify him as someone most in need of a friend.

Short-Term Objective

Joe will identify at least one student as a friend, and when a social survey is given in May, 30% or fewer of his classmates will identify him as someone they don't like to spend time with and 40% or fewer will identify him as someone most in need of a friend. At least one student will identify him as someone they would most like to do things with.

Annual Goal #2:

Joe will recognize and report bullying and teasing when it occurs, supervising school staff interventions will match his reports, and he will experience a decrease in bullying experiences.

Short-Term Objective

Teachers will report an increase in Joe's self-reporting of bullying incidents, an increase in adult interventions related to his reports, and an overall decrease of bullying to three times a week or less by December 31.

Short-Term Objective

Teachers will report that Joe is self-reporting when bullying occurs, school staff interventions match his reports, and the overall incidence of bullying is decreased to once a week or less by June 1.

Special Services Provided:

Provide individual instruction by (counselor, resource teacher, psychologist or other staff to be determined by school resources and established relationships) during fifth hour every other day to help promote skills for social competence and bullying prevention.

Provide a social lunch group twice a month facilitated by the (insert staff resource here).

Provide a "home base" and identify a "safe person" who will be available to Joe when he is stressed or anxious. (A "home base" is a designated place with a positive environment that the student can choose to go to when needed. A "safe person" is an adult that the student with AS is comfortable with; ideally, the adult supervising home base; Myles & Adreon, 2001, pp. 83, 85-86).

At least one monitor trained in AS will be available at lunch and recess to intervene immediately when bullying and teasing is most likely to occur.

Unique strategies would be developed based on the specific needs of the student, which might include direct instruction of social skills and calming strategies along with a variety of other individualized interventions such as teaching the student how to recognize bullying and strategies that will help provide for his safety. (The "Ten Bullying Strategies for Kids with Asperger Syndrome" in the Appendix provide a good foundation to help students with AS deal with bullying.)

It is essential that teachers receive training specific to the needs of students with AS. Some students may require provisions for educating other students about AS. Others may require occupational therapy services to address sensory needs to help manage stress and anxiety. Some students with AS may also need services through speech and language that focus on conversational skills or require help with anger management to find replacement behaviors to deal with their frustration and anger when they are bullied and teased. Similar strategies and interventions can be provided for a student with disabilities in general education by utilizing a 504 Plan.

None of these interventions can take the place of proactive adults intervening when bullying occurs, bullies changing their behaviors, and bystanders stepping up to make a positive difference in their school community. We have already discussed how adults can be more proactive in changing the school climate; let's explore more about how to help students identify their roles in bullying prevention.

Helping Students Identify Their Roles

One way of helping all students identify their role in bullying prevention is to discuss what it means to have courage and to recognize the different levels of support that students can provide to one another. Many students are afraid in our schools today. They are afraid to tell if they are being bullied and afraid to stand up when others are being bullied instead of standing passively by. Many students who witness bullying don't know what to do in response.

Bystanders

One student who witnessed a sixth-grade boy being bullied and harassed by an eighth grader in the locker area during passing time compared it to witnessing a car wreck:

> *Everything happens so fast, sometimes you aren't sure how to react and by the time you figure out what is going on, you have already passed on by, so you assume someone else will help. You don't want to stare but you can't look away. You are afraid of being late for class, afraid of saying something stupid, afraid of being the next target, afraid of getting hurt, and honestly relieved it isn't you getting bullied. You feel sort of sad, scared, and anxious when you see someone else getting hurt and then you feel guilty for not doing anything about it. The next time you go by the lockers, you are worried that someone will bother you.*

Many students struggle with what to do about bullying and with the code of silence that is often honored, especially in middle and high school when peer pressure is at its peak. We can help students who witness bullying by discussing ways they can assist students who are being bullied and the different levels of support they can give – ranging from not joining in, walking away, standing by but not participating, getting help from adults, and recruiting other peers to stand up against the bully. At a higher level of risk, students can individually stand up for the target and help him or her get away from the situation, verbally stand up to the bully, privately support the target, befriend or include the target, or stand up and chastise the bully in front of other peers (Garrity et al., 2000).

Bullies

Adults need to help students who bully examine their role by helping them recognize their behaviors as inappropriate, establishing limitations for their behavior, promoting empathy, and directing their energies into more positive, acceptable endeavors. The ideal result would be that students who bully use their desire for power and influence to be a positive role model and leader in their school community before their bullying patterns become so embedded that they experience life-long consequences in their relationships.

Targets

Students who are targeted for bullying require a considerable amount of support, as already discussed. Targets of bullying need adults at home and school to be proactive when bullying occurs so they can learn to trust and predict that there are adults they can rely on to help them and then learn to seek out their help. These students also need adults to model appropriate behaviors and teach them social competence that will help them become more self-confident. Specifically, they need to learn how to cooperate with others through problem-solving and conflict resolution skills so they can learn to build better relationships. Building these relationships will hopefully result in them being alone less and thereby decrease their vulnerability to being targeted by students who bully. The role of targets is to do what they can to make things better for themselves without feeling blame for being bullied.

Conclusion

Individualizing strategies for students who bully, bystanders, and students targeted by bullies is an important part of any bullying prevention program. General strategies can be used successfully with many students; however, the needs of student with AS require modifications or even totally different strategies and interventions. Teachers and parents also need to remember that siblings of students with AS may be targeted for bullying related to their brother or sister.

As emphasized throughout this book, bullying must be examined from a developmental and environmental perspective. There are no easy answers. Adults should not make the mistake of thinking bullying is too complex of a problem to deal with, but neither should we minimize the impact bullying behaviors have on our children.

Even preschoolers and children in elementary school can come into contact with many people during the course of their day. Teachers, paraprofessionals, health professionals, other children's parents, peers, people at the grocery store, zoo, and other public places, and the child's own nuclear and extended family can and will impact how children view themselves. Children are constantly given feedback on how others perceive them. Bullying can happen in the classroom, at recess, in the hallways, at other people's houses, in a neighbor's yard, on the way to and from school, or any place where people interact with each other. Bullies come in all sizes and ages; sometimes they include the very adults our children are instructed to respect and obey.

In order to impact the effect bullying has on the lives of children, we must not allow ourselves to become overwhelmed with the enormity of the task. Many times persistent, seemingly small efforts can have a major impact. On the other hand, we must not delude ourselves into thinking that the world our children live in is small and manageable. Particularly in dealing with children diagnosed with AS, this reinforces the literal, black-and-white thinking that these children are so prone to already. We need to prepare children to deal with a variety of social challenges and be careful not to feed into their naïvety and inflexibility by promoting the belief that if they are "good and kind," others will always be their friends and/or treat them with kindness in return. This misconception will make them even more vulnerable to being manipulated by others who may not have their best interest at heart.

This is especially true in bullying situations where children make friendly overtures to others but actually intend to "set them up," manipulate, or humiliate them in some way. We can help children be accepting and kind without making them so vulnerable. Children (including children with AS) will be better served by our efforts to help create a more tolerant, caring environment, but also a community where students are held accountable for their actions toward others. No child after gathering the courage to tell an adult that she is being bullied should hear, "I can't believe (insert child's name) would do that."

Adults must provide children with clear expectations for behavior and the information and skills they need in order to become caring, tolerant persons. All children need to receive guidance on social skills and conflict resolution and to see socially appropriate behaviors and attitudes modeled by the adults in their lives.

All children need to receive guidance on social skills and conflict resolution and to see socially appropriate behaviors and attitudes modeled by the adults in their lives.

If parents and school staff recognize bullying behaviors in themselves first and foremost, and work proactively to create a learning environment where bullying behaviors are clearly defined and consistently addressed, they will be able to greatly impact the environment where children spend the majority of their time. This change in attitudes and behaviors will then filter out past the school walls into our homes and beyond. Adults must lead and take responsibility for creating this safer environment and also help provide children with the skills they need to be safe and to feel socially connected.

If we only focus on teaching strategies to children who are bullied, our efforts will fail. If we only punish the children who bully, we will also fail. If we expect students to follow the philosophy of "Do as I say and not as I do," our actions will always speak louder than our words. Instead, we must have the conviction and courage to "do the right thing."

A young man who has experienced a great deal of bullying in his life wrote the following poem. Ben is 16 years old and diagnosed with AS. He introduces his poem by saying ...

> *"I enjoy writing poetry to express my feelings. 'With Sword in Hand' is a poem that reflects my feelings about getting the courage to stand up for myself and for what I believe. I hope by reading this poem, you will find courage to stand up for yourself and what is right."*

With Sword in Hand

With sword in hand, thy blade shines bright
In the midst of the eerie moonlight
I'll withstand this evil that creeps in the night.

With sword in hand, the darkness fades
Away into the sea of graves

Forever they will stay
Away,
From the shining light of day

With sword in hand, my fear fades away
For today, I fear nothing
Which always gives me something
My sword is called Courage
And Courage is what saves me
From those who haunt thee.

With sword in hand, thy blade shines, forevermore.

– Ben L.

CHAPTER 11

Personal Perspectives on Bullying*

This chapter presents a variety of perspectives on bullying. As many different views as possible have been represented to offer a comprehensive view of bullying. Professionals, including a director of a student advocacy center and a private practice psychologist specializing in social processing, as well as parents of children diagnosed with AS, and personal perspectives from people of different ages diagnosed with AS provide insights on bullying and the unfortunate impact it has on individuals, families, schools, and our society as a whole. Some of the commentaries reflect the resiliency of the human spirit and provide hope for the future. I hope you will be as touched and inspired as I have been by the courage and honesty of those who have chosen to share their personal insights and experiences.

* Except for minor editing for consistency in style, statements are reprinted as submitted.

Middle School Anyone?

Richard Howlin, Ph.D.
Chelsea Center for Learning and Development
Chelsea, Michigan

As a psychologist specializing in social processing, I have attempted to support many children with Asperger Syndrome (AS) through the social jungle of school. Middle school is by far the most troublesome and, for many children, the worst of times. On some occasions the classic pattern of "predator" bullying behavior has been apparent. The child with AS is targeted for a variety of reasons, including timidity, outspokenness, weak physical stature or academic ability.

Perhaps one of the most difficult realities faced by parents and caring adults is the fact that we often find ourselves powerless in the social arena of our children. Intimidation occurs at many levels, and when children step into the school environment, they are instinctively aware of how separate and challenging this world can be.

Protecting children from hostile behaviors of peers should, I believe, be a concern shared by adults. Schools must overtly address these issues and seriously pursue instances of harassment and bullying. This does not, however, guarantee acceptance and tolerance at more subtle levels. These behaviors reflect the character and culture of the peer population and their home environments. In a macro pop culture where clothing is accepted as the main criterion for acceptance or rejection by many circles of teenage girls, we have a serious problem. Culture, character, and behavior are frequently dictated by popular images beyond the classrooms. In shopping malls and television music shows, teens are continually exposed to an early sexual emphasis and countless fads. Such influences are typically not conducive to positive character traits and emphasize superficiality and sexual attraction above all else.

Thus, concerned educators, teachers and parents have to somehow negotiate this enormous backdrop in the politics of the classroom. In my own experience with the social lives of children with AS, I have found that one of the most potent supports through the difficult early adolescent years can be found in friendship or interest groups. Many children with AS are oblivious or unconcerned about the latest fad or in-group. Their interests rather than social impressions frequently drive their wish for contact and camaraderie. Thus, providing groups for interests and exchange is a potent force against alienation. This is an intervention that is relatively simple to implement. Examples include chess and science clubs.

Along with helping the children who struggle to find their social niche, we must also continue to foster character development in all children. Beyond the media culture lie real and fundamental human needs and concerns. Helping children on the autism spectrum adapt and develop social competence is a key concern. However, as adults we must also confront the destructive distractions that infect the social behaviors of all children.

"Access Denied"

Ruth Zweifler
Executive Director
Student Advocacy Center of Michigan

Foreword to *Access Denied: Mandatory Expulsion Requirements and the Erosion of Educational Opportunity in Michigan* (1999). Ann Arbor: Student Advocacy Center of Michigan, p. iii. Used with permission.

Amidst the swirling debates about school reform and school choice, the waning commitment to universal education is scarcely noticed. Belief in the essential importance of an informed electorate to a vibrant democracy has been replaced by allegiance to an increasingly elitist and exclusionary society. Not only our children but our public education system is at great risk.

In Michigan, mandatory expulsion requirements (zero tolerance) have taken on a life of their own. In addition to those weapons, rape, and arson offenses identified under the recent mandatory section of the Michigan School Code, more and more districts are removing children for vague offenses with vague criteria for length of exclusion and arbitrary and uncertain criteria for reentry. Justifications of these actions are a muddle of mandatory language and, until recently, rarely used Michigan School Code language that allows for expulsion for gross misdemeanor or persistent disobedience. In neither case is there a requirement to provide alternative education, other necessary supports, or supervision.

Every expulsion is, by law, a permanent action, although parents may petition a school board to consider readmission. Children who are expelled for weapons offenses must remain out of school for at least one year unless they are in kindergarten through fifth grade, in which case they may ask to be reinstated after six months. Children expelled for other than weapons violations may apply for readmission at any time. In any case, there is no requirement or guarantee that a school board will approve the request for admission. Reinstatement under all circumstances studied appears to occur less than 50 percent of the time.

The mandatory expulsion law was marketed as a way to stop dangerous "punks," older adolescents with guns. In reality, instead of netting sharks, the law and its attendant policies and practices are catching minnows – young children who are often frightened, sometimes thoughtless, rarely dangerous, but now clearly endangered.

Miranda's Mom
Michigan

Miranda has been excluded from games and other activities, overtly teased, intimidated, and outcast throughout her preschool and primary education. While she has never been completely friendless, her social challenges have been great. It has been a painful, confusing journey for Miranda, who has emerged, at the age of 10, with low self-esteem and feelings of hopelessness. Looking back through the last seven and a half years, I have many regrets about the way I responded to these episodes and their resulting fallout. I wish I had been more proactive, more involved, and more aggressive. I wish I had asked for help.

Eleven months ago, Miranda was diagnosed with Asperger Syndrome (AS). With this new understanding I felt better prepared to help Miranda navigate the social milieu, to advocate more effectively for her within the school, and to help her achieve a greater understanding of herself. I am sorry to say that prior to the diagnosis, I was reluctant to reach out to the school for assistance, fearful that they would think Miranda's difficulties were a result of poor parenting. Having no other children at the time, I assumed we must have been doing something terribly wrong.

Miranda's exclusion from social gatherings, parties, and cliques has been an ongoing source of distress for her. In third grade, significant difficulties began involving a group of about four girls who were friends.

One of these girls was also a member of Miranda's Girl Scout troop (I'll call her "Rhonda"). Rhonda and Miranda got along well during Girl Scout activities, and seemed to genuinely appreciate each other's company. However, another girl in this group of friends (I'll call her "Jamie") was responsible, in part, for Miranda's refusal to go to school in the third grade. During third grade, Jamie had teased Miranda daily. She told Miranda that she looked like a pig and said, "When you were born, your first word was oink." Jamie did not want to include Miranda in her group, and told the other girls that if they talked to or played with Miranda, she would no longer be their friend. Miranda reported that on days when Jamie was absent, she would be included in the activities of the group.

Another girl in her class, whom Miranda had an on-again/off-again friendship with, came to school with invitations to her sleepover party one day. When Miranda asked her why she wasn't invited, the girl replied, "My parents say that you're a crybaby, and they don't want to deal with you on an overnight." During third grade Miranda received only one party invitation. In fourth grade she received none.

Walking to and from school, Miranda became a target for teasing and bullying. A boy on the Safety Patrol team teased Miranda relentlessly about the beret that she wore. He called her "Pepe Le Pew," and seemingly went out of his way to taunt her. One day, after school, a couple of neighborhood classmates followed Miranda home and were hiding and calling out to her. It was obvious to me that these kids were trying to trick Miranda, but Miranda was laughing and calling back to them, "Where are you guys?" She didn't understand that their intentions were not to involve her in their play but to make her the butt of their joke.

On the school playground, Miranda became the subject of ridicule by an older girl. Apparently, this girl took great pleasure in loudly mocking Miranda and making fun of her hair and clothing. I didn't know about this until I heard it from one of her classmates who informed me that this girl was "super mean." Miranda spent most of her recess periods alone, on the swing. I will always remember the awful, empty sadness I felt when I went to pick Miranda up from school during recess and witnessed her isolation first-hand. It was devastating for Miranda because she so desperately wanted friendships and to be included.

Toward the end of her fourth-grade year, shortly after receiving the Asperger diagnosis, we decided to transfer Miranda to a different school. Here, new kids took up the torment where the other kids left off. During an ice cream social that Miranda attended with her father, a classmate set

Miranda up. She approached Miranda, who was happily dancing to the live music, and told her that a group of girls wanted to see her dance. Miranda followed the girl over to the group and proceeded to dance in front of them. The girls laughed and made fun of her. When she realized that she was being made fun of, Miranda ran screaming to her father that she had to leave immediately. This same girl continued to torment Miranda for the remainder of the year.

We contacted the principal, who subsequently contacted the girl's parents. Thankfully, the episodes stopped. Now that Miranda is in fifth grade, this child has again made it her mission to make Miranda feel badly. During gym class she cheered when Miranda was assigned to a team other than her own, and made fun of Miranda's singing during vocal music. Again, we had to contact the school. Thankfully, Miranda was switched into a new gym rotation where she no longer encounters this child. At the start of this year, Miranda reported that when she would sit down at a table, the other girls would get up and leave. Miranda has managed to make one friend this year, and as this relationship has developed, her social circumstance has improved somewhat.

Unfortunately, these are only a small sampling of Miranda's encounters with bullies. I am even aware that one of Miranda's teachers contributed to her status as a target for intimidation by humiliating her in front of her classmates. As a parent, some of these offenses are easier to forgive than others. I find myself feeling sincere disdain for the most deliberate offenders, although they are only children. It is not something I feel good about, but I would not be honest if I pretended I felt otherwise. Children who avoid Miranda or choose not to play with her are easier to understand. Miranda has social learning differences that affect her ability to interact with her peers. Some of her behaviors inspire rejection. However, the behaviors of these other children have sometimes inspired in Miranda the desire to die or disappear. She has expressed this openly during times of great anguish, and has even said, "I am God's greatest mistake." It has often inspired her refusal to attend school and the battle that follows to get her there. Sending my child into such an unfriendly environment has been one of the most difficult things I have had to do. My instinct is to protect her at all costs; my intellect knows she must go.

Miranda is one of the bravest people I know. Her courage inspires my deepest respect. I often wonder at what cost she endures these indignities, and I grieve. I love you, sweet Miranda Jane.

Benjamin L.
Sixteen-Year-Old Diagnosed with AS
South Dakota

I have had a lot of experiences in the bullying area, and this is what I know:

1. The Bully – the abuser. The Bully picks on the Victim just to hurt, humiliate, and give the Bully an edge over his chosen Victim. The Bully is a tormentor. The Bully tries to prove that he is bigger and stronger and that the Victim will always remain weaker than the Bully.

2. The Victim – the one being picked on by the Bully. The Victim does not know why the Bully is abusing him. If the Victim fights back physically, not only will the Bully lose in a fight, so will the Victim. The Victim should only fight back mentally by talking to a schoolteacher or parent about the Bully conflict. That parent or teacher can help find ways to solve this kind of problem.

If you are being picked on, try running away from the Bully as fast as you can and don't look back. If there are two or more Bullies (we'll call this a gang if there are more) harassing you, scream as loud as you can to call for help. A police officer or someone else you know might be nearby and may hear your screams and come to bail you out of the situation.

Sometimes there might not be any help. This is why it is usually best to have a good friend walking home with you. That way, if your tormentor comes up to you and pushes you around, you can signal your friend to go get help. If your friend says he'll get help but does not come back, then he is afraid and may not be a true friend. If this happens, try to make a run for it and scream for help along the way. True friends help each other through situations. They don't abandon their friends and leave them hurting. They get help nearby in these situations.

The Bully will only keep picking on you if you do not do any of these things. If you decide not to do those things, you remain an open target for torture. It is best to talk problems out, not fight them out.

Talking your problems out is the best thing to do, even though you might not want to. When I was bullied a long time ago, I usually "shelled up." I never spoke to my parents about my problems at school.

Those were disastrous times in my life. I do not wish for another person to feel the pain that I felt. I only wish for others to be safe from Bullies. If you have had problems similar to my own, or maybe even different than mine, find a way to let an adult that you trust know that you need help.

Amanda L., Benjamin's Mom
South Dakota

Our eldest son, Ben, will soon be 17 years old. He is doing well in school. He enjoys spending time with his dogs and horses. He is brilliant with a computer and is an accomplished writer. He has friends. He is happy.

Our other son, Ethan, is 12. He is doing well in school. He enjoys spending time with his friends and he plays the flute beautifully. He loves our dogs. He is a great cook. He is happy.

Today, we are a family rich with love. I wish I could tell you that we always were. The truth is that our lives haven't always been this way. There was a time not long ago, when just about every aspect of our personal lives was a horrible mixture of chaos, turmoil, hatred, sadness, emptiness and pain.

Ben was a child who had some major challenges, as well as some amazing strengths. He didn't fit into any special group of kids at school. He had a very difficult time communicating. He did things differently than most of his peers, and the friends that he had in grade school deserted him when they entered junior high. As if that wasn't enough to deal with, he now had eight classes a day, a locker to deal with, noisy crowded hallways to navigate, assignments to keep track of. Yet, absolutely no one recognized that he needed help managing this huge transition.

Ben was not fitting in anywhere. We, the people who were supposed to guide and protect him, ignored all the signs that he was in a crisis and beginning to shut down. When he ran away from the school after being dropped off, I would pick him up and take him into the school myself. When he had violent outbursts, we punished him. When he had five to seven hours of homework, it seemed natural to put everything else in our lives on hold in order to explain the assignments to him. When he cried, we told him that we knew junior high was a tough time, but we all have to go through it. "Tough it out," we would say, "it's not going to kill you." During this whole ordeal we thought that he just needed to get through it. He needed to toughen up!

Four months into the school year, our son finally had enough. He was tired of the demands that he couldn't meet, insults he couldn't defend, torture that he had no way of escaping. Everyone in his world expected him to be something or someone he just wasn't capable of being.

On a winter day on my way to a sign language class that is taught a few blocks from our house, I saw Ben walking home from junior high. When I stopped and asked how his day had gone, he told me that it was fine, but he had gotten into some trouble with another student and that he had a note from the principal for me to sign. I told him not to worry too much about it, that we would sort it out after my class.

When I got home, Ethan, who was 9 years old at the time, was standing on the sidewalk, no shoes or coat, Game Boy in one hand and his other hand on his head. He was screaming and sobbing at the same time. As we went inside, he told me that Ben had kicked him in the head, because he would not let him have the Game Boy. Ethan's head looked bad, and he was hysterical. I took him to a neighbor, who had been a nurse. He examined Ethan, checked his pupils, and told me to watch for sleepiness, pupil dilation, vomiting, etc. Then Ethan and I returned home.

After sending Ethan to our bedroom, I confronted Ben, who began by screaming the "hows" and "whys" that would make Ethan responsible for this incident. Our lives had become so chaotic that episodes like this happened quite a bit. But this time was different; Ben was enraged. Talking didn't help. In fact, it made things worse. As his rage escalated, I continued to try to get Ben to understand how very wrong his behavior had been. We began pushing each other and screaming, each wanting the other to relinquish control.

It was at this point that I realized how desperately we needed help. I began to calm down. Explaining to Ben that I thought we had better call some type of counselor or a crisis line, I went into the kitchen and picked up the receiver. Seemingly from out of nowhere Ben grabbed the phone from my hand, and as I tried to talk to him in a calm voice, he ripped the cord out of the wall. When I went on to explain why we needed to make the call, Ben reached into a drawer and pulled out a steak knife.

At this point everything happened so fast, yet remembering it, it seems as if it happened in slow motion. I called to Ethan, who met me in the hallway. In one motion I picked up Ethan and headed for the front door. As I struggled to open the first door, I turned to see Ben less than three feet away, moving toward us with the steak knife raised over his head. He had locked both the front door and the storm door. While Ethan screamed, I fumbled with the lock on the storm door. Tripping over the dog, Ethan still in my arms, I stumbled down the front step and ran next door. The police were called and Ben was taken to the local hospital.

An entire year went by before we learned the exact nature of what our son's life was like at school. Ben was finally able to tell us that a boy had been calling him names on that horrible January day. Ben's reaction had been to yell at the boy and jam a pencil into his back. We didn't get a phone call from the school. We never did get the note Ben had brought home.

During that year our son was in four different institutions. He had four separate diagnoses and was turned away by 22 treatment centers from across the country, including our own state hospital.

Asperger Syndrome is no longer a mystery to us. At this time the majority of our difficulties are due to the challenges we face within our community. Some people have been very kind and extremely helpful. I will always be grateful for their generosity. Others have not been nearly as kind or helpful. Dealing with bullies and social injustice is an ongoing process for us. It can be challenging. The good news is that the very same strategies that work for our kids, work for adults too! Bullies can be challenging to deal with at any age. With practice I've found that it gets easier.

One lesson I've learned in this short time is that ordinarily kind and considerate people can be misinformed and misguided. I've learned that predatory children who torture others are everywhere and that we as adults must protect their potential victims. I've learned that sometimes it's a good idea to go to school with your child, even if he is in junior high. After our son was reintegrated, he was still having behavioral challenges. Only by going to school with him did I learn of the abuse he was suffering.

After hours of research, running off copies of strategies, countless IEP meetings, and a two-hour inservice, not one change had been made in the way things were done. The emotional, environmental, educational, cognitive, language and positive behavioral strategies Ben was using to recover were completely ignored. Schoolmates were still picking on him. One boy, whom Ben was expected to sit next to in two classes, had been suspended for slamming books down on the desk behind Ben just to watch him jump. We were never notified. It was a concerned teacher who told me about this and other incidents the day I went to school with Ben. Ben didn't have the power to tell us, and those who could have helped him did nothing. He never went back to that school.

Personally, I've learned that I have the power to do anything I set my mind to. This is a new feeling for me. I didn't plan on it. It is a totally unexpected benefit of working alongside Ben as his partner, interpreter, protector and friend.

Peter Myers
Artist and Adult Diagnosed with AS
York, England

From my own experience, I wonder to what extent an individual should be compelled to meet the needs of the environment, and to what extent the environment should accommodate the needs of the individual. I don't believe it is a "cut and dry" issue, but one that depends on the individual and individual circumstances.

I believe in "inclusion." However, I feel that inclusion should mean "inclusion," not mere lip service to the concept. Putting an individual into an environment and not providing the necessary supports merely creates a social dumping ground, which is tantamount to exclusion. I would even term it a form of abuse or discrimination. Individuals may be doing their level best to conform to demands, but may find themselves forced beyond their own levels of physical, mental, and emotional endurance. I recall years of almost constant, almost intolerable anxiety in school.

There is structured and unstructured time and play, getting to school by 9:00 AM, going home at 4:00 PM, and learning what the lessons are and when (once one has one's bearings). Time in between, apart from "running the gauntlet of the corridors," is usually called a rest period, break, or "playtime."

"Playtime" at school is to allow children time to relax, or "burn off" surplus energy. However, it was neither conducive to my relaxation (high levels of anxiety), nor how I "burn up" surplus energy.

Children, I noticed, ran around a lot, made a lot of noise, competed with another, thumped, kicked, head butted, or even spat. I noticed they would take jackets and ties off when hot – something they would ridicule me for not doing, even when sweating profusely. I had no idea why they would steal, lie, intimidate, and fight, bully, or just generally physically, mentally, or emotionally abuse. But I know I did not like it.

"Playtime" I found a nerve-racking experience. I tended to avoid it if at all possible. In school I was a "milk monitor." That way I avoided play prior to school starting, as I got to school early and set the milk out for the other children. During the remainder of the school break periods, I would help my teacher prepare for lessons, thus staying inside and avoiding "play" (I did this with my friend Graham, with whom I got "joint class prize" in the final year).

In high school I again attempted to avoid "playtime," by joining the Biology Club and Film Society. With the Film Society I could watch films (e.g., *Dr. Strangelove*) during lunch breaks, and with the Biology Club I could stay in the biology lab, tend to my charge (looking after stick insects), and experience the safety, security, peace and quiet of that room.

However, due to the behavior of disruptive children (causing flooding in the bathroom, theft, arson, vandalism), the headmaster, who seemed unwilling or unable to maintain order, decided to punish all children by having all of us thrown out of the school building at break periods. It may have helped if the play areas were supervised, but quite often this was not so. Basically unruly children unsupervised "ran riot" with none of the safety checks one would expect in a well-run school.

I had lost my place of safety and quiet. I no longer had a tranquil environment in which to "recharge my batteries" prior to the stress of lessons. I found myself a prisoner of the schoolyard. I was not allowed out of the school grounds, nor inside the safety of the school buildings. I was in No Man's Land, a hostile environment, where the pack ran free and sought its prey.

I was ideal prey. I am passive and will not fight, even to defend myself. I was a figure of fun. I was a prime target, a soft target, and an easy target. I was an object of physical, mental, and emotional abuse. It did not last a day, week or month; it continued day in, day out for five years.

The only defense I could muster was to try not to be provoked, as this would only intensify matters and make them worse, and to keep as low a profile as possible. I was never beaten up at school, but this was not due to the lack of other children trying to provoke a situation where this could happen. I find it quite incredulous that a person who is known to have a reputation for passivity should provoke an opposite reaction in others.

I did not leave school unscathed. Half a decade of daily humiliation, ridicule, abuse, and torture left me with considerable feelings of low self-esteem. I am very introverted. When much younger, I was more extroverted, focusing things more outwardly, as in a tantrum. I think, because the outside world was such a difficult place for me to function in, I became increasingly reliant on my pre-existing introverted aspect of self.

Extroverts focus energy outwardly; introverts tend to focus energy inward on self. As a result of the anger and frustration from my experience of school, I focused on self, and this became depression. The drawings I did at that time are very similar to those I have seen by children who experience manic depression, although I tend not to have mania, being more hypo, than hyper in nature. The depression I experienced from school tends not to go away. I find it is cyclical in nature. I left school and over a quarter of a century later, I still carry the scars today.

The torturers are gone physically. Perhaps now they have families of their own. Perhaps now they are different personalities, nice, polite, down-to-earth people. For myself the "ghosts" of these torturers remain in my depression and low self-esteem.

One of the most surprising things I have learnt is that the biggest, baddest torturer or demon is an aspect of self. It can tear apart or rip asunder a thousand times worse than the real perpetrators of crime against humanity, and I know it will persist until a person can cease to play the victim of the past in the present. It is a battle I fight today, just as I fought those internal battles – not to fight, not to be provoked – so long ago.

Unlike some who look back at their schooldays as "the happiest days of their lives," when I left school, it was not with any regret, but relief! What I thought about my days of schooling was, "If I can survive this, then I can survive anything!" Yet if I had to face it all again, and while being aware of the toll I would pay in an endeavor to retain this special aspect of self, then I consider the price a small one.

"Those that do not learn from the past are doomed to repeat it." I want to contribute, take part, participate, but feel I am being impeded from doing so. If my experiences can help others, make their life easier, increase their quality of life, give them a chance, then it gives my life meaning and makes it worthwhile. I know that others on the autism spectrum have cried out for a voice to be heard. In common, we experience "self-ism," but we may not lack sympathy for another, or others like ourselves.

References

American Psychiatric Association. (1994). *Diagnostic and statistical manual of mental disorders* (4th ed.). Washington, DC: Author.

Aronson, E. (2000). *Nobody left to hate: Teaching compassion after Columbine.* New York: Henry Holt and Co.

Atlas, R., & Pepler, D. J. (1998). Observations of bullying in the classroom. *American Journal of Educational Research, 92,* 86-99.

Ayers, W., Dohrn, B., & Ayers, R. (2001). *Zero tolerance: Resisting the drive for punishment in our schools.* New York: The New Press.

Bashe, P., & Kirby, B. (2001). *Oasis guide to Asperger Syndrome: Advice, support, insights, and inspiration.* New York: Crown Publishers.

Batsche, G. M., & Knoff, H. M. (1994). Bullies and their victims: Understanding a pervasive problem in the schools. *School Psychology Review, 23,* 165-174.

Bender, W. H., Shubert, T. H., & McLaughlin, P. J. (2001). Invisible kids: Preventing school violence by identifying kids in trouble. *Intervention in School and Clinic, 37*(2), 105-111.

Bieber, J. (Producer). (1994). *Learning disabilities and social skills with Richard Lavoie: Last one picked ... first one picked on.* Washington, DC: Public Broadcasting Service.

Brown, D. (n.d.). *Inventory of wrongful activities.* Retrieved August 1, 2002, from http://www.safeculture.com/iowa.html.

Cline, F., & Fay, J. (1992). *Parenting teens with love and logic: Preparing adolescents for responsible adulthood.* Colorado Springs, CO: Pinon Press.

del Barrio, C., Gutierrez, H., Hoyos, O., Barrios, A., van der Meulen, K., & Smorti, A. (1999). *The use of semistructured interviews and qualitative methods or the study of peer bullying.* Retrieved November 25, 2002, from http://www.gold.ac.uk/tmr/reports/aim2_madrid1.html.

Fay, J., & Funk, D. (1995). *Teaching with love and logic: Taking control of the the classroom.* Golden, CO: The Love and Logic Press, Inc.

Foltz-Gray, D. (1996, Fall). The bully trap: Young tormentors and their victims find ways out of anger and isolation. *Teaching Tolerance*, 18-23.

Forero, R., McLellan, L., Rissel, C., & Bauman, A. (1999). Bullying behaviour and psychosocial health among school students in New South Wales, Australia: Cross sectional survey. *The British Medial Journal, 319*, 344-348.

Frey, K. (2000). Second step: Preventing aggression by promoting social competence. *Journal of Emotional and Behavioral Disorders.* Retrieved September 4, 2002, from http://www.findarticles.com/

Fried, S., & Fried, P. (1996). *Bullies and victims: Helping your child survive the schoolyard battlefield.* New York: M. Evans and Company, Inc.

Gagnon, E. (2001). *Power cards: Using special interests to motivate children and youth with Asperger Syndrome and autism.* Shawnee Mission, KS: Autism Asperger Publishing Co.

Garbarino, J., & deLara, E. (2002). *And words can hurt forever: How to protect adolescents from bullying, harassment, and emotional violence.* New York: The Free Press.

Garrity, C., Jens, K., Porter, W., Sager, N., & Short-Camilli, C. (2000). *Bully-proofing your school: A comprehensive approach for elementary schools.* Longwood, CO: Sopris West.

Gianetti, C., & Sagarese, M. (2001). *Cliques: 8 steps to help your child survive the social jungle.* New York: Broadway Books.

Graham, S., & Juvonen, J. (2001). An attributional approach to peer victimization. In J. Juvonen & S. Graham (Eds.), *Peer harassment in school: The plight of the vulnerable and victimized* (pp. 49-72). New York: Guilford Press.

Hair, E., Jager, J., & Garrett, S. (2002). Helping teens develop healthy social skills and relationships: What the research shows about navigating adolescence. *Child Trends Research Brief.* Retrieved March 30, 2003, from http://www.childtrends.org/PDF/K3Brief.pdf.

Hazler, R. J., Carney, J. V., Green, S., Powel, R., & Jolly, L. S. (1997). Areas of expert agreement on identification of school bullies and victims. *School Psychology International, 18*, 5-14.

Heinrichs, R. (2003). A whole-school approach to bullying: Special considerations for children with exceptionalities. *Intervention in School and Clinic, 38,* 195-204.

Hoover, J. H., Oliver, R., & Hazler, R. J. (1992). Bullying: Perceptions of adolescent victims in the Midwestern U.S.A. *School Psychology International, 13,* 5-16.

Howlin, P., Baron-Cohen, S., & Hadwin, J. (1999). *Teaching children with autism to mind-read.* Chichester, England: John Wiley & Sons.

Howlin, R. (2002). *Understanding Asperger Syndrome (social dyslexia).* Retrieved January 29, 2002, from http://www.aspergersmichigan. com/asperger.html.

Jeffrey, L.R., Miller, D., & Linn, M. (2001). Middle school bullying as a context for the development of passive observers to the victimization of others. *Journal of Emotional Abuse, 2* (2/3), 143-156.

Johnson, D. W., & Johnson, R. (1991). *Teaching students to be peacemakers.* Edina, MN: Interaction Book Co.

Kavale, K. A., & Forness, S. R. (1996). Social skills deficits and learning disabilities: A meta-analysis. *Journal of Learning Disabilities, 29,* 226-237.

Little, L. (2002). Middle-class mothers' perceptions of peer and sibling victimization among children with Asperger's Syndrome and nonverbal learning disorders. *Issues in Comprehensive Pediatric Nursing, 25,* 43-57.

Maslow, A. (1987). *Motivation and personality* (3rd ed.). (R. Frager, J. Fadiman, C. McReynolds, & R. Cox, Eds.). New York: Addison-Wesley Educational Publishers Inc.

Myles, B., & Adreon, D. (2001). *Asperger Syndrome and adolescence: Practical solutions for school success.* Shawnee Mission, KS: Autism Asperger Publishing Co.

Myles, B., & Southwick, J. (1999). *Asperger Syndrome and difficult moments: Practical solutions for tantrums, rage, and meltdowns.* Shawnee Mission, KS: Autism Asperger Publishing Co.

Nansel, T., Overpeck, M., Pilla, R., Ruan, W., Simons-Morton, B., & Scheidt, P. (2001). Bullying behaviors among U.S. youth: Prevalence and association with psychosocial adjustment. *Journal of the American Medical Association, 285,* 2094-2100.

National Association of Attorneys General. (2000). *Bruised inside: What our children say about youth violence, what causes it, and what we need to do about it.* Retrieved March 20, 2002, from http://www.naag.org.

O'Connel, P., Pepler, D., & Craig, W. (1999). Peer involvement in bullying: Insights and challenges for intervention. *Journal of Adolescence, 22,* 437-452.

Olweus, D. (1993). *Bullying at school: What we know and what we can do.* Oxford: Blackwell Publishers.

Pepler, D., & Craig, W. (1999). What should we do about bullying: Research into practice. *Peacebuilder, 2,* 9-10.

Pepler, D. J., & Craig, W. (2000). *Report 60: Making a difference in bullying.* LaMarsh Centre for Research on Violence and Conflict Resolution. Retrieved March 30, 2002, from http://pavlov.psyc.queensu.ca/~craigw/makediff.pdf.

Perry, D. G., Hodges, E.V.E., & Egan, S. K. (2001). Determinants of chronic victimization by peers: A review and a new model of family influence. In J. Juvonen & S. Graham (Eds.), *Peer harassment in school: The plight of the vulnerable and victimized* (pp. 73-104). New York: Guilford Press.

Polakow-Suransky, S. (1999). *Access denied: Mandatory expulsion requirements and the erosion of educational opportunity in Michigan.* Ann Arbor: Student Advocacy Center of Michigan.

Rigby, K. (1996). *Bullying in schools: And what to do about it.* London: Jessica Kingsley Publishers.

Robinson, S. M. (1999). Meeting the needs of students who are gifted and have learning disabilities. *Intervention in School and Clinic, 34,* 195-204.

Salmon, G., James, A., & Smith, D. M. (1998). Bullying in school: Self-reported anxiety and self-esteem in secondary school children. *British Medical Journal, 317,* 924-925.

Schwartz, D. (2000). Subtypes of victims and aggressors in children's peer groups. *Journal of Abnormal Child Psychology, 28,* 181-192.

Schwartz, W. (1999). Developing social competence in children. *Choices Briefs.* Retrieved March 20, 2002, from http://iume.tc.columbia.edu/choices/briefs/choices03.html.

Simmons, R. (2002). *Odd girl out: The hidden culture of aggression in girls.* New York: Harcourt Books.

Simpson, R. L., & Myles, B. S. (1998). *Educating children and youth with autism: Strategies for effective practice.* Austin, TX: Pro-Ed.

Smith, P. (1991). The silent nightmare. Bullying and victimization in school peer groups. *The Psychologist, 4,* 243-248.

Swearer, S. M., Song, S. Y., Cary, P. T., Eagle, J. W., & Mickelson, W. T. (2001). Psychosocial correlates in bullying and victimization: The relationship between depression, anxiety, and bully/victim status. *Journal of Emotional Abuse, 2,* 95-121.

Talbot, M. (2002). Girls just want to be mean. *The New York Times on the web.* Retrieved March 6, 2002, from http://www.nytimes.com/2002/02/24/magazine/24GIRLS.html.

Tanguay, P. B. (1999). *Cooperative learning and the NLD student.* Retrieved March 1, 2003, from http://www.nldontheweb.org/tanguay_2.htm.

Thompson, M., Cohen, L., & Grace, C. (2002). *Mom, they're teasing me: Helping your child solve social problems.* New York: Ballantine Books.

Thompson, M., Grace, C., & Cohen, L. (2001). *Best friends, worst enemies: Understanding the social lives of children.* New York: Ballantine Books.

Troy, M., & Sroufe, L. A. (1987). Victimization among preschoolers: Role of attachment relationship history. *Journal of Child and Adolescent Psychiatry, 2,* 166-172.

U.S. Code. (1994). *Federal Gun-Free Schools Act of 1994,* Sec. 8921 (20). Washington, DC: Author.

Vossekuil, B., Fein, R. A., Reddy, M., Borum, R., & Modzeleski, W. (2002). *The final report and findings of the safe school initiative: Implications for the prevention of school attacks in the United States.* Washington, DC: U.S. Secret Service and U.S. Department of Education

White, E. (2002). *Fast girls: Teenage tribes and the myth of the slut.* New York: Scribner.

Wiseman, R. (2002). *Queen bees & wannabes: Helping your daughter survive cliques, gossip, boyfriends, & other realities of adolescence.* New York: Crown Publishers.

Ziegler, S., & Pepler, D. J. (1993). Bullying at school: Pervasive and persistent special issues: Violence in the schools/schooling in violence. *Orbit, 24,* 29-31.

Resources

In choosing the resources listed in this section, I used the following criteria: strategies and programs validated through research, program availability – some resources are readily available on the Internet – flexibility, and being closely related to key components of bullying prevention. Also, I looked for resources that could be easily modified and individualized for children and adolescents with Asperger Syndrome (AS). Finally, some resources were chosen because they were specifically created for children with AS. I believe this list will provide parents, educators, and other professionals with adequate resources related to bullying prevention and intervention and may be useful in pointing to other resources and topics not specifically identified here.

Behavior/Anger Management

Effective Behavior Support (EBS) Program

This program takes a whole-school approach to dealing with problem or challenging behaviors in the school setting and is devised to help students learn more appropriate behaviors.
Institute on Violence and Destructive Behavior
College of Education
1265 University of Oregon
Eugene, OR 97403-1265
Email: ivdb@darkwing.uoregon.edu
Website: http://www.uoregon.edu/~ivdb/

Larson, J., & Lochman, J. (2002). *Helping schoolchildren cope with anger: A cognitive-behavioral approach.* New York: Guilford Press.

This book presents the Anger Coping Program, an empirically supported intervention for anger and aggression issues.

Myles, B. S., & Southwick, J. (1999). *Asperger Syndrome and difficult moments: Practical solutions for tantrums, rage, and meltdowns.* Shawnee Mission, KS: Autism Asperger Publishing Company.

This book is an indispensable resource for parents and professionals trying to understand and respond to typical behavioral and emotional responses that can occur when working with individuals with Asperger Syndrome and related disorders. It contains many practical strategies for use in the home, school, and community. http://www.asperger.net.

Nambka, L. (1997). *The dynamics of anger in children.* Retrieved April 2, 2002, from http://members.aol.com/AngriesOut/teach6.htm.

This article discusses the relationship between anger and social skills deficits and, therefore, is helpful for those who live and work with individuals who have AS.

Bullying Programs

Bonds, M., & Stoker, S. (2000). *Bully-proofing your middle school: A comprehensive approach.* Longwood, CO: Sopris West.

This book presents a whole-school approach to establishing and implementing a bullying prevention program. It is very comprehensive and addresses a critical age group, middle school students. http://www.sopriswest.com.

Garrity, C., Jens, K., Porter, W., Sager, N., & Short-Camilli, C. (2000). *Bullyproofing your school: A comprehensive approach for elementary schools.* Longwood,CO: Sopris West.

This book presents a whole-school approach to establishing and implementing a bullying prevention program and includes many reproducible forms. It is very comprehensive and has a strong focus on empowering bystanders. Many of the strategies are appropriate for students with AS; others can be easily modified for these students. http://www.sopriswest.com.

Gray, C. (2000). Gray's guide to bullying part I: The basics. *The Morning News, 12*(4).

Gray, C. (2001). Gray's guide to bullying part II: The real world. *The Morning News, 13*(1).

Gray, C. (2001). Gray's guide to bullying part III: How to respond to a bullying attempt. *The Morning News, 13*(2).

This special three-part series offers information on bullying and children with autism spectrum disorders. It can be ordered from The Gray Center for Social Learning and Understanding, http://www.thegraycenter.org.

The Bullying Appendix provides practical activities and ideas along with a guide to children's books related to bullying and self-esteem. This resource is available at http://www.thegraycenter.org.

Heinrichs, R. R. (2003). A whole-school approach to bullying: Special considerations for children with exceptionalities. *Intervention in School and Clinic, 38*(4), 195-204.

This article provides insights about the vulnerability of students with exceptionalities and the dynamics of bullying in schools. It includes practical interventions at the school, class, and individual level.

Olweus' Core Program Against Bullying and Antisocial Behavior (also know as the Bullying Prevention Program)

For more information, visit the Center for the Study and Prevention of Violence (CSPV) at the University of Colorado website at http://www.colorado.edu/cspv/blueprints/model/programs/BPP.html. You may also contact:
Dan Olweus, Ph.D.
University of Bergen
E-mail Olweus@psych.uib.no

Or:
Susan Limber, Ph.D.
Institute on Family and Neighborhood Life
Clemson University
E-mail slimber@clemson.edu

This program is a whole-school approach to bullying prevention. Based on Olweus' work, which is the model for many other programs, it has been thoroughly researched and has proven effective in bullying prevention.

Olweus, D. (1993). *Bullying at school: What we know and what we can do.* Oxford, UK & Cambridge, USA: Blackwell Publishers.

This book provides indispensable information about bullying and Dr. Olweus' research, which has influenced most, if not all, other bullying prevention programs.

Steps to Respect

This is a bullying prevention program with a dual focus on bullying and friendship. It takes a whole-school approach to bullying and is an excellent resource. http://www.cfchildren.org/strres.html.

Conflict Resolution

Peace Education Foundation (PEF)

The mission of this non-profit educational organization is to educate children and adults about conflict and to encourage peacemaking skills throughout schools, families, and communities. The program consists of six components, conflict resolution, mediation, parent component, suspension/detention, bus drivers, and implementation. The suspension/detention section provides alternatives to typical suspension and detention. The section on bus drivers provides a comprehensive program for empowering bus drivers with training and education related to conflict. This is an affordable resource for schools. http://www.peaceeducation.com.

Resolving Conflict Creatively Program (RCCP)

RCCP is a research-based K-12 school program in social and emotional learning. The primary goal of the program is to help young people develop social and emotional skills that will help reduce violence and prejudice and promote caring relationships and healthy lives. The philosophy of the program is to change school cultures so these skills are modeled and taught with as much emphasis as the other basic educational subjects.

More information can be found at the Educators for Social Responsibility website at http://www.esrnational.org/.

Or contact:
Jennifer Selfridge
RCCP Program Director
Email: jselfridge@esrnational.org

Or:
Linda Lantieri
RCCP Founding Director
Email: llantieri@rccp.org

Resolution Vocabulary

This is a list of terms and definitions related to conflict resolution. Retrieved February 21, 2003, from http://www.teachervision.com/lesson-plans/lesson-2991.html.

Educational

Cumine, V., Leach, J., & Stevenson, G. (1998). *Asperger Syndrome: A practical guide for teachers.* London: David Fulton Publishers.

This is an effective guide for teachers and other professionals who support individuals with Asperger Syndrome and related disorders.

Gagnon, E. (2001). *POWER CARDS: Using special interests to motivate children and youth with Asperger Syndrome and autism.* Shawnee Mission, KS: Autism Asperger Publishing Company.

This book shows parents and educators how special interests can be used in a unique, yet practical way to help motivate children with autism spectrum disorders. http://www.asperger.net.

Moore, S. T. (2002). *Asperger Syndrome and the elementary school experience: Practical solutions for academic & social difficulties.* Shawnee Mission, KS: Autism Asperger Publishing Company.

This book is full of strategies that can help promote success in the school environment for elementary-age students with Asperger Syndrome and related disorders. http://www.asperger.net.

Myles, B. S., & Adreon, D. (2001). *Asperger Syndrome and adolescence: Practical solutions for school success.* Shawnee Mission, KS: Autism Asperger Publishing Company.

This is a tremendous resource for educators and parents related to school issues. http://www.asperger.net.

Myles, B. S., & Simpson, R. L. (2001). Effective practices for students with Asperger Syndrome. *Focus on Exceptional Children, 34*(3), 1-14.

This is a comprehensive resource for educators who advocate for students diagnosed with AS and related disorders. It contains many practical strategies that can be taken directly to the classroom.

Safran, J. (2002). Supporting students with Asperger's Syndrome in general education. *TEACHING Exceptional Children, 34*(5), 60-66.

This article is an excellent, practical resource for educators working with students diagnosed with Asperger Syndrome and related disorders. http://www.aspennj.org/articles.html.

Online Lesson Plans

Family Education Network

Offers resources for addressing violence in school as well as free lesson plans for teaching conflict resolution. The Learning Network offers an array of online educational tools, content, and resources. http://teachers.infoplease.com.

Online lesson plan about bullying and school violence for grades 6-8. Retrieved April 4, 2003, from http://school.discovery.com/lessonplans/programs/cruelschools/cruelschools.rtf.

This comprehensive lesson plan is free of charge. Handouts are also available online to use with the lesson plan.

Online lesson plan about cyberspace including ethical issues for grades 9-12. Retrieved April 4, 2003, from http://school.discovery.com/lessonplans/programs/cyberspace/cyberspace.rtf.

This comprehensive lesson plan is free of charge. Internet use is an important topic of discussion and paves the way for a discussion of cyberspace bullying and safety issues.

Online curriculum for exploring the rewards and challenges of cyberspace including bullying situations and personal comfort levels while on the Internet. http://www.cybersmartcurriculum.org.

The curriculum involves discussions of comfortable and uncomfortable feelings and how to handle the unacceptable behavior of others while on the Internet. Activity sheets include bullying scenarios, feeling uncomfortable, recognizing bullies, and strategies for taking action. This is an extremely important topic for discussion, as the Internet is quickly becoming a major vehicle for bullying.

Families

Bullying information for teens. Retrieved April 3, 2003, from http://www.safeyouth.org/teens/topics/bullying.

This document, specifically written for teens, provides an introduction to bullying and strategies for dealing with bullying when it occurs. Helpful links and resources are also given.

Bushman, B., & Anderson, C. (2001). Media violence and the American public: Scientific facts versus media misinformation. *American Psychologist, 57*(6/7), 477-489.

Children Now. (2001). *Fair play: Violence, gender, and race in video games.* Retrieved April 3, 2003, from http://www.childrennow.org/media/video-games/2001/#violence.

This article presents a comprehensive study of all types of videogames and the effects on the children who play them. It provides an abundance of information to parents who may have concerns about the type of videogames and/or the amount of time their children play such games. This is a pastime enjoyed by many children, including many children with Asperger Syndrome and related disorders.

Helping your children navigate their teenage years: A guide for parents. Adapted from: White House Council on Youth Violence. (2000). Retrieved April 3, 2003, from http://www.mentalhealth.org/publications/allpubs/SVP-0013/SVP-0013.pdf.

This guide assists parents in dealing with issues that typically occur during the teenage years. It is a good resource for helping parents look at their adolescent's behavior and attitudes within a normal developmental framework as a way to prepare for social and peer influences during the teenage years.

Health Professionals

Bullying Information for Health Professionals
Retrieved March 30, 2003, from http://www.safeyouth.org/faq/hc/hcg.htm.

This document contains information on bullying designed specifically for health professionals. It outlines how health professionals can help address the problem of bullying in their community.

Coleman, W. L., & Lindsay, R. L. (1998). Making friends: Helping children develop interpersonal skills. *Contemporary Pediatrics.* Retrieved April 5, 2003, from http://www.contpeds.com (put "bullies" in site search).

Garrity, C., & Baris, M. A. (1996). Bullies and victims: A guide for pediatricians. *Contemporary Pediatrics.* Retrieved on April 5, 2003, from http://www.contpeds.com (put "bullies" in site search).

Both of the articles from *Contemporary Pediatrics* are excellent resources for health professionals and families. They discuss concrete ways that pediatricians, other health professionals, and parents can advocate for their children related to bullying and friendship skills.

Miscellaneous

Everyday Hero
Retrieved January 25, 2003, from http://www.ksu.edu/wwparent/
programs/hero/

This program is particularly suited to children with AS because of the strong use of animal metaphors, which is often an area of interest for children with AS. The concrete representation of abstract concepts helps promote understanding. The program establishes roles and motivation for bystanders as well. Targeted to provide information to parents, teachers, and other caregivers of 10- to 12-year-old children, the program focuses on five critical elements of heroism: awareness, care, intelligence, strength, and action. The entire program is available at the website, with supplemental supplies available at a nominal charge.

Myles, B. S., Cook, K. T., Miller, N. E., Rinner, L., & Robbins, L. A. (2000). *Asperger Syndrome and sensory issues: Practical solutions for making sense of the world.* Shawnee Mission, KS: Autism Asperger Publishing Company.

This book addresses the issue of sensory needs and is therefore an excellent resource for parents, educators, and others who support individuals with AS and related disorders. http://www.asperger.net.

Social Skills

Alar, N. (2001). *Tips for running a social group (or, I was a cruise director in another life).*
Retrieved February 2, 2003, from http://www.asw4autism.org/ausome/
tips.htm.

This article provides a wealth of information about starting and running a social group for teenagers and young adults with autism spectrum challenges.

Baker, J. E. (2003). *Social skills training for children and adolescents with Asperger Syndrome and social-communication problems.* Shawnee Mission, KS: Autism Asperger Publishing Company.

This excellent resource focuses on social skills that commonly cause problems for children and adolescents with Asperger Syndrome. Each skill is presented in a handy format, with the skill to be learned on one page and related activities on the facing page. http://www.asperger.net.

Big Brothers/Big Sisters
http://www.bbbsa.org.

This one-on-one mentoring program for young people has been proven to be associated with an increase in quality of the parent-child relationship. To my knowledge, the program has not been specifically researched for children with AS; however, there is no reason to think that it would not be equally effective with this group, especially if the mentor were educated regarding characteristics of children with AS. This type of mentoring relationship creates a wonderful opportunity for modeling social skills in a more natural environment.

Tierney, J., Grassman, J. B., & Resch, N. L. (2000). Making a difference: An impact study of *Big Brothers/Big Sisters.* Retrieved April 2, 2003, from http://www.ppv.org/content/reports/makingadiff.html.

This document provides further information about research results related to the impact Big Brothers/Big Sisters has on those who participate.

Connections Center

The Connections Center, founded by Dr. Steve Gutstein and Dr. Rachelle Sheely, offers a multidisciplinary program to develop evaluation and intervention programs for people with relationship disorders. A specific program has been designed for people on the autism spectrum to help them enjoy and develop meaningful relationships with others.
The website, http://www.connectionscenter.com, provides more information about the programs and books specifically intended for individuals on the autism spectrum.

McAfee, J. (2002). *Navigating the social world: A curriculum for individuals with Asperger's Syndrome, high functioning autism and related disorders.* Arlington, TX: Future Horizons Inc.

This curriculum is specifically designed for individuals with autism spectrum disorders and related disorders. The curriculum is comprehensive and can be equally helpful to parents, educators, and other professionals who work with individuals on the spectrum. http://www.futurehorizons-autism.com.

Moore, S. T. (2002). *Asperger Syndrome and the elementary school experience: Practical solutions for academic & social difficulties.* Shawnee Mission, KS: Autism Asperger Publishing Company.

This book devotes an entire chapter to information about various strategies and programs that can be used to help individuals with AS or related disorders develop social skills. http://www.asperger.net.

Second Step

This prevention program provides a whole-school approach to curbing aggression and fostering social competence in children preschool through grade nine. Committee for Children http://www.cfchildren.org.

Also:
Frey, K. (2000). Second step: Preventing aggression by promoting social competence. *Journal of Emotional and Behavioral Disorders.* Retrieved September 4, 2002, from http://www.findarticles.com/cr_0/mOFLB/2_8/62804298/print.jhtml.

Useful Websites

Asperger Syndrome

Asperger Information
http://www.aspergerinformation.org

Asperger Syndrome Coalition of the U.S. (ASC-US)
http://www.asperger.org/index_asc.html

Asperger Syndrome Educational Network, Inc. (ASPEN)
http://www.aspennj.org/

ASPIRES/Asperger Syndrome Partners & Individuals Resources,
Encouragement and Support
http://www.justgathertogether.com/aspires.html

Autism Asperger Publishing Company (AAPC)
http://www.asperger.net

Autism Society of America
http://www.autism-society.org

IDEAPractices/Professional Development Resources
http://www.ideapractices.org/resources/
This website provides an incredible amount of information on a variety of educational issues. Many publications published by the U.S.
Department of Education, Office of Special Education Programs, are
available online and provide empowering information for parents and
professionals.

Online Asperger Syndrome Information and Support (O.A.S.I.S.)
http://www.udel.edu/bkirby/asperger

The Source/Maap Services, Inc.
http://www.maapservices.org

Bullying

Anti-Bullying Network
http://www.antibullying.net/

Asperger Information
http://www.aspergerinformation.org

Bullying.org… "Where you are NOT alone"
http://www.bullying.org/

Center for the Study and Prevention of Violence
http://www.colorado.edu/cspv/

Committee for Children
http://www.cfchildren.org/resources_parent.shtml

Cyberbullying
http://www.cyberbullying.ca

Kansas Bullying Prevention Program
http://www.kbpp.org

Online Bullying Help Center for K-12 Schools
http://www.bullystoppers.com

Take Action Against Bullying
http://www.bullybeware.com/

Appendix

Ten Bullying Strategies for
Kids with Asperger Syndrome

1. Keep telling adults when you are bullied or teased. Find out who will listen to you and take action.

2. If you are being bothered at recess, stay closer to an adult and play with or around other kids when you can.

3. If someone is bothering you and won't stop, say, "Stop that" loudly, turn around quickly, and walk away.

4. As you walk away, try to remember who you see standing around; they may be a witness to what happened.

5. Say something assertive like "Back off," instead of attacking back by saying something mean like "You're an idiot, too."

6. If someone asks you to do something or say something to someone else you don't feel right about, stop, think, and say, "Why don't you do it yourself," then don't do it!

7. Stay away from kids who are mean to you and don't keep trying to make them like you no matter how popular they are.

8. Talk to and hang around with kids who are nicer to you but may not be as popular as others; they may need a friend.

9. If someone tells you to stop doing something, they probably mean it. So stop.

10. Watch kids who usually get along with most everyone, including the teachers, and see how they act in different situations. You might get some good ideas for how to behave.

Straight Talk About Bullying

I am a nurse, special education teacher, parent, and author of a book called *Perfect Targets: Asperger Syndrome and Bullying: Practical Solutions for Surviving the Social World.* I want to talk to you about bullying. I am going to be very honest and get to the point. I know that you probably are being bullied or that you have been bullied some time in your life. I know that some kids call you names, play tricks on you, and don't include you in their games and activities. Sometimes they leave you out when they have birthday parties and talk about it right in front of you. I also know that sometimes you even get hit or hurt physically in other ways. I understand that you don't always tell your parents or teachers about some of the things that happen to you because you don't think you should or you don't think it will help. You might even believe that it will make things worse if you tell an adult. You think it isn't cool to tell because that is what you are taught to think by the other kids. Unfortunately, you may have found that sometimes when you ask for help from adults, they disappoint you.

I know that often when you are with other kids you wonder why they seem to pick on you more than on anyone else. It sure seems that way to you. Sometimes when you think someone is trying to be nice to you, they end up laughing *at you.* You don't always know why, but you can usually tell when someone is laughing at you. Even when you realize other kids aren't being very nice to you, sometimes you put up with it or do or say things to get their attention so you can feel like part of the group. This kind of makes you feel bad, but not as bad as being totally left out. Some days are really hard, aren't they? I mean those days when you feel like everything you say is wrong but you don't know why, and then you get mad and things just keep getting worse.

I want to tell you a few things that I know for a fact are true. It is not your fault that you are being bullied and teased. As a matter of fact, lots of kids are bullied and teased every day, including kids who don't have Asperger Syndrome. It is not their fault either. The truth is, some of the kids who bully have been bullied themselves either at home or at school. Some of them are popular and seem to have everything going for them and bully because they like how it makes them feel. What they don't know is that sooner or later people won't like them if they keep it up and they won't want to spend time with them, because the truth is, nobody really likes a bully.

There is something else you need to know. The reason there is so much bullying in schools is that adults aren't doing enough to stop the bullying. It is their job. Sure there are things you can learn that can help keep you safe and maybe even help make some of the bullying stop. You see bullying is all about power. Bullies want power and they don't care if they have to hurt someone else to get it. Adults are the ones who have the power to stop bullying because they are the ones in charge.

The sad truth is, some adults don't realize (or remember) how bad it feels to be bullied. The good news is that there are adults in every school that get it! They can and will help. Your job is to keep telling adults about the bullying until you find the adults who understand and will help. I promise you that if you keep asking for help, you will get help.

Don't forget about your parents. Sometimes parents get upset when you first tell them about the bullying, but they aren't upset with you even if they start telling you what you need to do to make it stop. Parents just get a little, or a lot, emotional at first because they care so much about you. They can help if you talk to them and let them know what is going on.

Sometimes it may seem to you that your parents should already know why you are upset. Sometimes it is hard to believe that teachers don't see what is going on. You may think they just don't care or that they think what the bully is doing is okay. Tell them anyway and tell them how it makes you feel. If you keep telling adults, you will find help. You don't have to put up with bullying. Don't start fights or become a bully yourself because it isn't safe and it won't help. It will make things worse and it will make you feel bad about yourself.

Don't believe that you just have to "take it" either. Don't believe that it isn't cool to tell. That is a lie that other kids tell to stay out of trouble. Tell adults in private whenever possible. If you are being bothered at recess, stay closer to the teachers. Yell, "Stop it" if someone is really bothering you and turn around and walk away. Look around for other kids who might have seen what happened and try to remember who they are. They might be able to tell an adult what happened.

Don't hang around with the kids who are really mean to you, thinking you can do something to make them like you. Look for kids who maybe aren't as popular as others but treat you better. Maybe you can become friends. Don't waste your time on kids who bully unless THEY CHANGE! Most of all, remember to keep talking to adults; they've got the power to help and you have the power to get help. If you keep telling them, they will begin to understand and they will be able to help.

Rebekah Heinrichs
heinrichs@aspergerinformation.org

Modified Inventory of Wrongful Activities

Diagnosis: _____

Birth date: _____

Gender: (Circle or underline)   Male   Female

Today's date: _____

School: (Circle or underline)   Public   Private   Home school

Grade: _____

Please complete and return by mail or email to:

Rebekah Heinrichs
c/o AAPC
P.O. Box 23173
Shawnee Mission, KS 66283-0173

Email: heinrichs@aspergerinformation.org

Please email any questions regarding this inventory.
Thank you for your response.

No personal identifying information will be associated with your response.

Modified by Rebekah Heinrichs from the original Inventory of Wrongful Activities written by: Dennis Brown, safeculture.com, 802 North Lincoln, Creston, IA 50801; dbrown@heartland.net; 800-606-9750; Safe Culture© Project DB

Modified Inventory of Wrongful Activities

Has a student (or students) from your school done any of the following things to you?

CHECK ALL ITEMS that have happened to you THIS SCHOOL YEAR.

Someone has:

____1.   Pulled my hair, hit, pinched, kicked, tripped, bit, or spit on me

____2.   Torn my clothes or broken my things (such as pencil breaking)

____3.   Stolen from me

____4.   Scared me or threatened me with a weapon (like a knife or gun)

Someone has:

____5.   Said bad things about me (calling me names like "fat" or "freak")

____6.   Said bad things about my family (like calling my Dad a "wimp")

____7.   Written mean notes about me

____8.   Made me afraid to talk in class or make mistakes because of teasing

---

____9.   Asked me to do things that I get in trouble for doing (like saying something rude to the teacher)

____10. Scared or threatened me into doing something I didn't want to do (like giving up money or doing someone else's homework)

____11. Asked me to do things that make me uncomfortable (like telling me not to talk to certain people)

____12. Made it hard for me to learn in school because I feel scared, angry, sad, or upset about the way people treat me

____13. Made me not want to go to school because I feel scared, angry, sad, or upset about the way people treat me

Modified by Rebekah Heinrichs from the original Inventory of Wrongful Activities written by: Dennis Brown, safeculture.com, 802 North Lincoln, Creston, IA 50801; dbrown@heartland.net; 800-606-9750; Safe Culture© Project DB

____14. Left me out of a group or activity

____15. Made mean faces at me (like rolling eyes)

____16. Laughed at me to be mean

Someone has:

____17. Used hand signals to be mean (like making an "L" with their fingers and putting it on their forehead)

____18. Made fun of something they think is different about me (like being tall, short, wearing glasses, braces, or talking or walking differently)

____19. Insulted me because I am in a different class or program

____20. Insulted me or made jokes about my color or race

____21. Insulted my ability to learn in class

____22. Made fun of my clothes or my parents' car, house, or job

---

____23. Insulted me with sexual talk or jokes (could include hand signals like raising the middle finger or name-calling like "slut" or "fag")

____24. Spread sexual rumors about me (like telling people I am "gay" or "easy")

____25. Made me uncomfortable by taking off their clothes or "mooning" me ("mooning" is when someone exposes their bare buttocks to another person)

____26. Pulled (or tried to pull) my clothes off or down

____27. Grabbed, pinched, or kicked me in a private area

____28. Touched me in a sexual way without my permission (like kissing, hugging, putting hands on my private areas or holding me)

____29. Written sexual insults about me on walls, desks, or something else

Modified by Rebekah Heinrichs from the original Inventory of Wrongful Activities written by: Dennis Brown, safeculture.com, 802 North Lincoln, Creston, IA 50801; dbrown@heartland.net; 800-606-9750; Safe Culture© Project DB

The next three statements ask for your feelings about your teachers and their actions.

CHECK ALL ITEMS that are TRUE for you.

___30. I feel some teachers don't like me as well as other students

___31. I feel hurt or angry (once a week or more) about a teacher's actions or words

___32. I wish my teachers would stop someone who is acting mean to me

CHECK ALL ITEMS that are TRUE for you.

When are mean things said or done to you?

___33. Before school

___34. Between classes

___35. After school

___36. During classes

___37. At lunch time

___38. At after-school activities

CHECK ALL ITEMS that are TRUE for you.

What places should adults watch better to keep students from being mean to you?

___39. Hallways

___40. Bathrooms

___41. Classrooms

___42. Lunchroom

___43. Gym lockers

___44. Outside on school property

Modified by Rebekah Heinrichs from the original Inventory of Wrongful Activities written by: Dennis Brown, safeculture.com, 802 North Lincoln, Creston, IA 50801; dbrown@heartland.net; 800-606-9750; Safe Culture© Project DB

Choose ONLY ONE answer for these questions and WRITE THE LETTER on the line provided.

____45. Do people act mean to you on the school bus?

    A. I do not ride the school bus

    B. People **do not** act mean to me on the school bus I ride

    C. People **do** act mean to me on the school bus I ride

____46. What do **most of your teachers** do when they see students acting mean?

    A. They usually do nothing. They ignore it.

    B. They do very little. They might say, "Quit that."

    C. They make them stop and teach them not to act that way any more.

____47. What do you do when you see students acting mean to other students?

    A. I sometimes join in and act mean too.

    B. I do nothing. I ignore it.

    C. I ask people to stop acting mean. I try to stop it.

    D. I tell a teacher so he or she can help.

Choose ONLY ONE answer for these questions and WRITE THE LETTER on the line provided.

____48. What do you do when people are mean to you at school?

    A. I act mean right back.

    B. I do nothing. I ignore it or accept it.

    C. I tell them to stop.

    D. I tell a teacher so he or she can help.

____49. How often are people mean to you at school?

    A. Almost never

    B. Several times a week

    C. About once a day

    D. More than once a day

Modified by Rebekah Heinrichs from the original Inventory of Wrongful Activities written by: Dennis Brown, safeculture.com, 802 North Lincoln, Creston, IA 50801; dbrown@heartland.net; 800-606-9750; Safe Culture© Project DB

___50. How often do you tell adults at school when people are mean to you?

    A. I almost never tell

    B. I tell some of the time

    C. I tell most of the time

    D. I tell every time

___51. What usually happens when you tell an adult at school about someone being mean to you?

    A. It helps a lot

    B. It helps some

    C. It does not make a difference

    D. It makes things worse

___52. What usually happens when you tell your parents about someone being mean to you?

    A. It helps a lot

    B. It helps some

    C. It does not make a difference

    D. It makes things worse

CHECK ALL ITEMS that are TRUE for you.

Which adults at school do you go to for help when someone is being mean to you?

___53. Counselor

___54. Teacher

___55. School psychologist

___56. Principal

___57. Vice principal

___58. Resource teacher

___59. Para

___60. Resource police officer

___61. Other

Modified by Rebekah Heinrichs from the original Inventory of Wrongful Activities written by: Dennis Brown, safeculture.com, 802 North Lincoln, Creston, IA 50801; dbrown@heartland.net; 800-606-9750; Safe Culture© Project DB

Please include any additional comments here:

Modified by Rebekah Heinrichs from the original Inventory of Wrongful Activities written by: Dennis Brown, safeculture.com, 802 North Lincoln, Creston, IA 50801; dbrown@heartland.net; 800-606-9750; Safe Culture© Project DB

Index